AWAKENING INTUITION

About the Author

FRANCES E. VAUGHAN, Ph.D., is a practicing psychologist in Marin County, California. Formerly the president of the Association for Transpersonal Psychology, she is currently on the faculty of the California Institute of Transpersonal Psychology as well as on the Board of Editors of the *Journal of Transpersonal Psychology* and the *Journal of Humanistic Psychology*.

AWAKENING INTUITION

Frances E. Vaughan

ANCHOR BOOKS
Anchor Press/Doubleday
Garden City, New York

The Anchor Books edition is the first publication of AWAKENING INTUITION.

Anchor Books edition: 1979

Grateful acknowledgment is made for permission to reprint the following material:

Selected lines from "East Coker" from *Four Quartets* by T. S. Eliot. Copyright 1943 by T. S. Eliot and copyright 1971 by Esme Valerie Eliot. Reprinted by permission of Harcourt Brace Jovanovich, Inc.

Selected lines from "The Labyrinth" from *Collected Poems* by W. H. Auden. Copyright 1945 by W. H. Auden and renewed in 1973 by W. H. Auden. Reprinted by permission of Random House, Inc.

ISBN: 0-385-13371-5
Library of Congress Catalog Card Number 77-27685

PREFACE

Writing a book about intuition is truly paradoxical. Others, wiser than I, have rejected the impossible task of translating intuitive learning into the rational, linear language of words. But despite the fact that musicians, artists, poets, and others who use nonverbal forms of expression give more direct access to intuitive ways of knowing, many of us persistently feel the urge to communicate our experience, and attempt to use words to do so. Sharing the methods which helped me validate and expand my own intuition with hundreds of people in workshops and classes encouraged me to follow that urge, and this book is the result.

I had some difficulty writing in the third person. Originally I wrote as I would talk, shifting back and forth from first person, to second, to third. For the sake of consistency and readability, however, I have modified this, although I do not feel entirely comfortable with the impersonal style. I address you, the reader, as if you were in a workshop or seminar, and though at times this may sound didactic, it seems to be a way in which I can communicate clearly. Wherever I make statements about "one" I include myself; I felt "I" would be too restrictive, since I am attempting to discuss ideas that transcend the personal dimension of experience.

As you read this book, consider the exercises an invitation to explore for yourself some processes which others have found rewarding. You are ultimately responsible for what you do or do not choose to do, since I cannot know what is appropriate for you. You are free to pick and choose as you see fit, to accept or reject anything I say; you will recognize whatever is true for you. Awakening intuition is really about learning to trust yourself. My intention is simply to share with you some of the learning which has been meaningful to me in my life's journey.

In giving examples and recounting experiences shared by people in my workshops, I have changed the names of individuals and places in order to protect their privacy. I am grateful to all of you who have shared your intuitive experiences with me, both individually and in groups.

I am particularly indebted to Dr. Robert Gerard, who first introduced me to some of the exercises presented in this book, and who, five years ago, encouraged me to write a book about intuition. I also want to thank Jim Fadiman for his assistance in making this book a reality, and to acknowledge the many friends whose love and support have contributed to my work. I will not name you all, but you know who you are. And, for their special contribution to my life, this book is dedicated to my children, Robert and Leslie.

CONTENTS

In order to arrive at what you do not know
*   You must go by a way which is the way of igno-*
*   rance.*
In order to possess what you do not possess
*   You must go by the way of dispossession.*
In order to arrive at what you are not
*   You must go through the way in which you are*
*   not.*
And what you do not know is the only thing you know
And what you own is what you do not own
And where you are is where you are not.

—T. S. Eliot: *Four Quartets*

AWAKENING INTUITION

INTRODUCTION

Intuition is known to everyone by experience, yet frequently remains repressed or undeveloped. As a psychological function, like sensation, feeling, and thinking, intuition is a way of knowing. When we know something intuitively, it invariably has the ring of truth; yet often we do not know *how* we know what we know.

Popular interest in the development of mental powers has prompted many people to pay more attention to their latent intuitive abilities. Although everyone has intuition, it is more highly developed and more available to some people than others. It is, however, possible for everyone to awaken his or her own intuition and to use it both helpfully and profitably in everyday life. Learning to use intuition is learning to be your own teacher, and getting in touch with your own inner guru.

The role of intuition in creativity, problem solving, and interpersonal relationships is vital, yet it is frequently discounted and mistrusted by those who do not understand it. Many people are frightened by experiences which seem unusual, illogical, or paranormal, and therefore fail to make use of their intuition as a source of creative inspiration and reliable information about themselves and their environment. Almost everyone, however, by becoming more aware of how intuition works, and by giving careful consideration to the problems of its validation and interpretation, can make much fuller use of intuitive capacities.

Extrasensory perception, clairvoyance, and telepathy are part of the intuitive function. Likewise, artistic inspiration and mystical religious experience are intuitive perceptions of reality. Current brain research indicates that the left hemisphere of the brain is predominantly rational, linear, and verbal in its functioning, whereas the right hemisphere is predominantly intuitive, holistic, and oriented toward pattern perception. In recent years new methods have been developed for educating and training the neglected intuitive faculties.

In addition to opening one to the aforementioned experiences, developing the intuitive faculties allows one to recognize the possibilities inherent in any situation. When one becomes aware of possibilities, one is free to make choices. Choice is always available, but it becomes real only when one is conscious of having it; if choices in life are made automatically, or unconsciously, the experience of freedom remains elusive. Awakening intuition enables one to see the choices available and is thus a liberating experience. Before experiencing this liberation, however, one must first make a fundamental choice with respect to intuition itself—whether or not to give time and attention to its awakening.

This book presents a number of exercises designed to bring about a well-balanced integration of the rational and intuitive functions. They may or may not be of use to you; only you can judge. Consider the exercises an invitation to expand your experience by developing a greater awareness of what you already know. There is nothing you *have* to do to awaken your intuition; but if you choose to do the exercises they will work most effectively if critical judgment is temporarily suspended in order to allow intuition to emerge. Holding it in abeyance should not be confused with turning it off, however, as your rational, discriminating judgment is essential to checking the validity of intuitive perceptions and evaluating the process.

At any given moment one is conscious of only a small portion of what one knows. Intuition allows one to draw on that vast storehouse of unconscious knowledge that includes not only everything that one has experienced or learned, either consciously or subliminally, but also the infinite reservoir of the collective or universal unconscious, in which individual separateness and ego boundaries are transcended. This book provides a framework for the opening and exploration of that storehouse. For many, it will be an initiation; for those who already acknowledge and use their intuition, it will be a guide to integrating, affirming, and validating intuitive experiences in everyday life.

1

Tuning In to Intuition

> The truth, insofar as it can be stated in words, must always be a set of instructions on how to awaken the non-dual mode of knowing, therein to experience reality directly.
>
> —KEN WILBUR: *The Spectrum of Consciousness*

Everyone knows something about intuition. For some people, intuition is vital, familiar, and readily available. For others, it is a vague, undifferentiated faculty which may remain latent throughout life. Like musical talent or the capacity for logical thinking, intuition is naturally more developed in some people than in others, but it is potentially available to everyone. Some people choose to develop it, others do not.

If one chooses to pay attention to intuition, one can certainly expand awareness of it. Learning to awaken intuition, however, is paradoxical, since intuitive experiences tend to occur spontaneously and too much effort is apt to interfere with the process. Yet although one cannot *make* intuition happen, there is much that one can do to *allow* it to happen. Given this paradox, let us examine the best approach to awakening intuition.

First of all, it is a good idea to check your existing attitudes and beliefs about the subject. Are you willing to relinquish your attachment to figuring things out in order to experience another way of knowing? Ken Wilbur points out that the negation of thought is not nihilism, but the opening of non-dual insight, or the path of intuition.[1] "Stop thinking and talking about it," says the third Chinese patriarch of Zen, "and there is nothing you will not be able to know."[2] It is not easy, however, to stop thinking; for most people some form of thinking goes on, automatically, all the time. Do you believe it is possible to quiet your mind in order to expand your awareness of reality? Remember that if you do not believe it is possible you probably will not succeed in doing so, unless you are truly able to temporarily suspend your disbelief. Be honest with yourself. Lying to yourself about what you believe doesn't work. You may be able to deceive others, but at some level you always know when you are trying to deceive yourself. If you are uncertain or confused, simply acknowledge that this is where you are at the moment.

It is also a good idea to treat yourself with kindness and compassion. This does not mean you can just be lazy, "space out," or go to sleep; maintaining alert attention is essential to awakening. But too much effort generates resistance, and forced attempts at self-improvement are likely to be short-lived. Be prepared for disappointment if you think that the attainment of psychic powers will enable you to get anything you want thus solve all your problems. Awakening intuition is not about "getting more"; it is about "being more" who you really are. Thus, the first step in this process is learning to let yourself be.

If you are willing, you can begin by learning to relax. If you already know how to relax, or if you meditate, you may want to proceed directly to the concentration exercises which begin on page 20. The practice of meditation is one of the most direct methods of tuning in to intuition. Although there are many different methods used for teaching meditation, and states of consciousness achieved are by no means the same, all forms of meditation focus the mind and direct attention away from rational, analytical thinking and thus favor the development of intuition. Daniel Goleman suggests that at the point of awakening, it is likely that all meditative paths merge, or that at least the similarities among various systems far outweigh the differences. Describing the effects of this experience on the meditator, Dr. Goleman says: "As the states produced by his meditation meld with his waking activity, the awakened state ripens. When it reaches full maturity, it lastingly changes his consciousness, transforming his experience of himself and of his universe."[3] If as a meditator you have experienced such states, your intuition is no doubt already awakened. Assuming, however, that you are just beginning to explore the possibilities of awakening your intuition or would like to expand your awareness of it, this chapter is addressed to the prerequisite steps of learning to relax and focus attention.

Relaxation

Exercises for developing the concentration necessary for awakening intuition work best when they are combined with relaxation training. Eventually concentration or one pointedness of mind becomes effortless, but arriving at such a state requires considerable commitment. It is like developing any other skill. When you first try to ride a bicycle you may have a lot of difficulty balancing and staying on the bicycle. As you practice, however, it becomes easier and easier, until you are able to ride in a very relaxed way, and the tension you experienced at first completely disappears. Learning to focus your mind is always difficult at first, and pushing yourself too hard tends to generate resistance rather than speed up the process. Better results can be expected if you treat yourself as someone you love. If you wanted to teach someone you care for a valuable new skill, you would not berate the person every time he or she did not succeed, but would encourage progress by giving the person support and approval. Give yourself the same, and plenty of time to find out what works best for you.

Tension and anxiety interfere with learning of any kind. They not only impair concentration, but also block awareness of intuition at all levels. It is therefore important to find a method of relaxation which works for you and which you can use whenever you wish to quiet your mind. Learning to quiet the mind is essential to awakening intuition and also has many immediate benefits. Not only does it improve your ability to concentrate, it also allows you to feel more calm and relaxed in any situation and to remain centered amidst any internal or external turmoil. In the Hindu tradition, the undisciplined mind is likened to a drunken monkey; certainly the perpetual chatter that goes on in the mind most of the time is quite pointless, and a major obstacle to developing intuitive awareness. In any case, learning to relax and quiet the mind can make you feel better, function better, and maintain better health.

In practicing relaxation for the purpose of developing intuition, it is particularly helpful to choose a relaxation exercise which suggests an attitude of alert awareness and noninterference. Learning can be accelerated by using positive suggestions, but beware of too much conscious programing. Remember that you are learning to listen to what you already know, but that in order to hear, your mind must be quiet rather than full of the things you think you need to learn. A good way to begin the process of relaxing with conscious, noninterfering awareness is to pay attention to your breathing. Don't try to change it, just be aware of it. Breathing is one physiological function which goes on unconsciously all the time, and which can easily be brought into conscious awareness simply by attending to it. Easy as it is to be aware of your breathing, it may be difficult not to interfere with its natural rhythm as soon as you attend to it. Can you be aware of your breathing without altering it in any way? Notice the parts of your body that move when you breathe. Notice the parts of your body where you are holding on or interfering with the natural movement of the breath in some way. Don't try to change it, just be aware of it.

This simple exercise in breath awareness is the focus of various meditation practices. If you sit with your spine straight and simply attend to your breathing for a prolonged period of time, you will be able to learn a lot about the way your mind works. When your attention wanders and you find you have forgotten about your breath, simply return to that focus by bringing your attention back, gently and quietly, time after time. What requires effort at the beginning becomes effortless with continuing practice.

Although many relaxation techniques suggest lying down in order to facilitate complete letting go, for the development of intuition it is usually best to sit with your spine straight, as in meditation, in order to maintain mental alertness. Lying down tends to induce sleep, and that is not what you want. However, if you have trouble letting go and find that you cannot relax while sitting up, you may want to try lying down. Check your own responses and see what works for you.

One relaxation exercise taught in yoga is particularly appropriate here, as it suggests both activity and passivity and can be practiced either sitting up or lying down. Begin with your toes, and say to yourself: "I am relaxing my toes. My toes are relaxing." Continue to apply this awareness to all the different parts of your body:

> I am relaxing my feet. My feet are relaxing. I am relaxing my ankles. My ankles are relaxing. I am relaxing my calves. My calves are relaxing. I am relaxing my knees. My knees are relaxing. I am relaxing my thighs. My thighs are relaxing. I am relaxing my pelvis. My pelvis is relaxing. I am relaxing my buttocks. My buttocks are relaxing. I am relaxing my

back. My back is relaxing. I am relaxing my stomach. My stomach is relaxing. I am relaxing my chest. My chest is relaxing. I am relaxing my shoulders. My shoulders are relaxing. I am relaxing my arms. My arms are relaxing. I am relaxing my hands. My hands are relaxing. I am relaxing my neck. My neck is relaxing. I am relaxing the back of my head. The back of my head is relaxing. I am relaxing my forehead. My foreheard is relaxing. I am relaxing my eyes. My eyes are relaxing. I am relaxing my mouth. My mouth is relaxing. I am relaxing my jaw. My jaw is relaxing. I am allowing myself to be completely relaxed and I am at peace.

This exercise can be shortened or prolonged, depending on how you feel on a particular day. Sometimes it may suffice to spend only a few minutes consciously relaxing, while at other times, if you are particularly tense, you may want to go over the parts of your body in greater detail, inside and outside, giving yourself as much time and space as you need in order to reach a state of physical relaxation that will allow your mind to be quiet and clear.

Since part of the process of developing intuition is learning to tune in to the body and be alert to physical cues, in addition to learning to relax one can learn to attend to physical sensations without trying to change anything or interfere in any way. As in practicing breath awareness, it is sometimes difficult to be aware of physical sensations without altering them in some way. Any physical sensation which becomes the object of undivided attention does change. However, for the purpose of tuning in to intuition, the objective of attending to physical sensations is not to manipulate or control them, but simply to discover what they are.

Awareness Exercise

Take a few minutes to sit quietly and tune in to any physical sensations that are present for you at this

time. Don't try to change them, just be aware of
them. Notice the parts of your body that feel tense,
and notice the parts of your body that feel relaxed.
What parts of your body were you not aware of at all?
Keep your attention on your physical sensations for a
few minutes and notice anything that may come into
your awareness that was not there before.

Often you may be totally unaware of your body unless it
hurts. Yet your body can give you important messages
about what your needs are and what you can do to take
better care of yourself.

Open Focus Exercise

One of the most effective methods of combining body
awareness and imagination for deep relaxation and the
enhancement of intuitive faculties has been developed by
Lester Fehmi of the Princeton Medical Center. He calls it
the *Open Focus* exercise. It consists of a series of questions about your ability to imagine certain experiences
without making any effort to achieve them. Questions are
directed at evoking an "objectless image," namely distance
or space rather than a concrete object. According to Dr.
Fehmi,

> When one focuses awareness on space, one is left with the
> task of emptying or clearing objects from his imagery,
> broadening his focus, and moving in the direction of imagin-
> ing the dissolving or letting go of perceptions, i.e. "no-thing-
> ness." Specifically, imagining the space between points in
> the body or within specified body regions leads one to dis-
> tribute his focus equally over the region demarcated by ob-
> jective boundaries. It is the act of distributing or diffusing
> one's attention of a region, as opposed to narrowly focusing
> it upon a point, that gives rise to the states of consciousness
> and existence associated with reduction of anxiety, competi-
> tiveness, tension, inhibition, repression, and active goal-seek-
> ing behavior. While the logical extreme of narrow focus is
> one pointedness of attention, the logical extreme of open
> focus is a state in which diffusion of attention proceeds to

the point at which one loses self-consciousness, and also loses preoccupation with a sense of time. Thus, I refer to the latter extreme, but readily achievable, dissolved, and expanded state as "NO-TIME." Learning to flexibly vacillate between NO-TIME, less extreme states of open focus and narrow focus, and one pointedness of attention, as circumstances require, is a goal of OPEN FOCUS and biofeedback training. However, almost all persons thus far trained benefitted significantly from training which initially emphasized spending long periods in NO-TIME. Spending hours in the NO-TIME state is observed to be directly correlated with an increasing sense of well-being, the reduction of anxiety, tension and associated behaviors.

In giving instructions for beginning the exercise, Dr. Fehmi suggests:

. . . when I ask, "Can you imagine the space between your eyes?" you might naturally experience your eyes and then let your imagination flow to the region between your eyes and imagine the space between them. Your objective is not to come up with some number or other abstraction, such as, "There are two inches between my eyes." The objective is to very gently imagine or experience that space between your eyes. You initially may imagine or experience the space as a very small region or vague feeling, and the space might then grow or change as you continue between questions, and for that period I would like you to maintain your attention on the subject of the last question. If you have difficulty experiencing any particular image or experience, don't let that trouble you, just permit your imagination to remain oriented toward the object of the question and let nature take its course. If nothing particular seems to happen or your mind wanders, don't be disturbed. However, when the next question is asked, enter into the associated imagery. Finally, you needn't respond overtly in any way to these questions. Your response will be whatever happens to your imagery or experience when the question is asked.[4]

Can you imagine

—the space between your eyes
—the space between your ears

—the space inside your throat

—that the space inside your throat expands to fill your whole neck as you inhale

—the space between your shoulders

—the space between your hips

—the space between your thumb and first finger on each hand

—the space between your first and middle finger on each hand

—the space between your fourth and little finger on each hand

—that the region between the tips of your fingers and your wrists is filled with space

—that the region between your wrists and your elbows is filled with space

—that the region between your elbows and shoulders is filled with space

—that the region between your shoulders is filled with space

—that the space inside your throat is coextensive with the space between your shoulders and in your shoulders and arms, hands, and fingers

—that the regions inside your shoulders, and the regions between your shoulders and fingertips are simultaneously filled with space

—that your feet and toes are filled with space

—that the region between your arches and your ankles is filled with space

—that the region between your ankles and your knees is filled with space

—that the region between your knees and your hips is filled with space

—that the region between your hips is filled with space

—that your buttocks are filled with space

—that your buttocks and the region between your hips and your legs and feet and toes are simultaneously filled with space

—that your lower abdomen is filled with space

—that your lower back is filled with space
—that your body from the diaphragm down is filled with space, including your diaphragm, your genitals, your anus, and your feet and toes
—that the region between your navel and your backbone is filled with space
—that your stomach is filled with space
—that the region inside your rib cage is filled with space
—that the region between your ribs is filled with space
—the space inside your lungs as you inhale and exhale
—the space inside your bronchial tubes as you inhale and exhale
—the space inside your throat as you inhale and exhale
—the space inside your nose as you inhale and exhale
—the distance between the space inside your throat and the top of your head
—the distance between the space inside your throat and the space behind your eyes
—that the region between your temples is filled with space
—that your forehead is filled with space
—that your brain is filled with space
—that your spine is filled with space
—that your whole head is simultaneously filled with space
—that your whole head and your face are simultaneously filled with space
—that your whole head, face, neck, and your whole body, including your hands, genitals, and feet, are simultaneously filled with space
—that your whole being fills with air when you inhale and your whole being is left filled with space when you exhale
—At the same time that you are imagining the space inside your whole body, can you imagine the space around your body, the space between your fingers and toes, behind your neck and back, the space above your head and beneath your chair, and the space in front of you and to your sides

—that the boundaries between the space inside and the space outside are dissolving and that the space inside and the space outside become one continuous and unified space

—that this unified space, which is coextensive inside and outside, proceeds in three dimensions, front to back, right to left, and up and down

—that, at the same time you imagine this unified space, you can simultaneously let yourself attend equally to all the sounds that are available to you.

—that these sounds are issuing from and pervaded by unified space

—that at the same time you are attending to the space and the sounds you can also attend simultaneously to any emotions, tensions, feelings, or pains that might also be present

—that these sensations and perceptions are permeated by space

—that at the same time that you are aware of the space, the sounds, emotions, and other body feelings, you can also be simultaneously aware of any tastes, smells, thoughts, and imagery that might be present

—that you can now admit also to awareness any sensation or experience which may have been inadvertently omitted thus far, so that you are now simultaneously aware of your entire being, of all that is you

—that all your experience is permeated and pervaded by space

—that, as you continue to practice this open focus exercise, you will increase your ability to enter into open focus more quickly and more completely and more effortlessly

—that, as you continue to practice this open focus exercise, your imagery of space will become more vivid and more pervasive

—that, as you continue to practice this open focus exercise, your ability to imagine space permeating all of your

experience will continue to become more vivid and ever-
present

Concentration

The open focus exercise, by expanding awareness of
space, is excellent preparation for specifically focused exercises which use objects or symbols as devices to aid the development of concentration. The difficulty of keeping the
mind focused can be readily experienced by trying to hold
an image or an idea still for a minute or two. Let us now
turn our attention to the visualization of specific images
which aid the development of concentration and, in turn,
intuition.

The visualization of geometric forms, as practiced in
esoteric psychology,[5] is one way of strengthening intuitive right-brain functions. The following exercise, which
uses simple geometrical shapes as objects of concentration, gives you the opportunity to check your own powers
of concentration and acquaints you with the spontaneous
movement of imagery in the mind's eye.

Visualization of Geometric Forms

Close your eyes and imagine that you are drawing a
circle on a blackboard with white chalk. Make a white
dot in the middle of the circle. Imagine that the
image of the white circle with a dot in the middle on
a black background is suspended at the level of your
eyebrows, about a foot away, in front of you. Hold it
in your mind's eye for three minutes. Hold it perfectly still. Repeat the exercise using an equal armed
cross or plus sign in place of the circle. Again, imagine the cross to be white on a black background. If
you have difficulty visualizing it at first, imagine again
that you are drawing it on a blackboard with white
chalk. Hold this image for three minutes. Repeat the
exercise once more, using an equilateral triangle in

place of the circle and the cross. Again, visualize the figure in white on a black background, as if you had drawn it on a blackboard, and hold it still.

If you are trying this exercise for the first time and have not been previously trained in some form of meditation, you may be surprised to notice that the images are difficult to hold motionless. They may seem to take on a life of their own, changing color and shape and moving of their own accord.

You may prefer to simply watch what happens to the images in your mind, rather than exert the effort to keep them clear and still. This can be an interesting introduction to self-observation and a way of learning to watch inner images change and unfold without conscious, deliberate interference, but it is not the same as training the mind to focus on a single image and hold it still in the mind's eye. Learning to concentrate on a particular image is useful discipline. By continual practice one learns that one can indeed control one's thoughts and thus take responsibility for one's state of consciousness. Remember when you are beginning this practice that perseverance pays off, while impatience and too much effort only interfere with the ability to concentrate.

In this exercise concentration is active rather than passive, as it was in the open focus exercise. You can readily experience the different effects produced by these different approaches to developing concentration. When these exercises are practiced for the purpose of clearing away the obstacles to intuition, both are valuable. Allow yourself to experiment with different forms until you find one that suits you.

Word Concentration

Another approach to developing intuition through exercises in concentration is to use intuition itself as a focus of your attention. You can simply reflect on what intuition means to you, and try the following exercise.

When you are sitting quietly relaxed, simply hold the word INTUITION in your awareness. You may visualize the word written out before you, or you may simply repeat the word to yourself as if it were a mantra. Initially many extraneous thoughts and feelings are likely to intrude. Simply bring your attention back gently to the word INTUITION when you realize that your attention has wandered to something else. Many associations and unexpected insights may also appear spontaneously during such meditation and you may wish to record some of them after the meditation period is over. It is usually best to begin with brief periods of concentration (about five minutes, more or less) in order to avoid generating resistance and fatigue. Again, the key to amplifying your awareness of intuition is attention.

A participant in one of my workshops recorded her experience with meditating on intuition as follows:

> I began to listen to myself for the first time. I realized that there were many layers to my awareness, and I could get in touch with much deeper levels of myself. Superficial conflicts lost their importance and I found it easier to make decisions. It was as though I had gotten in touch with some inner guide, or sense of knowing. I no longer felt agitated and confused, but somehow more trusting of life itself as a process. The idea of allowing more of my experience to come into my conscious awareness without having to *do* anything to change it helped me learn to accept myself as I am.

Another way of working with the word INTUITION is to write down any associations you may have with the word. Associations should be brief. There is no need for explanation or amplification here; one or two words are enough. The word INTUITION should be written between each association. For example:

> Intuition knowing intuition seeing intuition feeling
> intuition understanding intuition consciousness
> intuition growing intuition space intuition timeless

intuition expansion intuition roots intuition flowing
intuition universal intuition beyond intuition tran-
    scendence intuition spiritual intuition earthbound
intuition rebirth intuition circle intuition natural
intuition colors intuition light intuition clear
intuition stars intuition deeper intuition centering
intuition letting go intuition trust intuition love
intuition letting be intuition acceptance intuition en-
    ergy
intuition giving intuition receiving intuition allowing
intuition movement intuition creating intuition ex-
    pectation
intuition living intuition being intuition . . .

If you keep going, allowing yourself to repeat words as
they occur to you and to be blank, or write *blank*, when
you feel it, you can get beyond the superficial associations
and closer to what the word really means for you. Don't
worry if your associations seem illogical. The point is *free*
association, which means letting anything come up, without judging it. As you uncover some of the deeper meanings which are there for you, you can clear away a lot of
preconceptions and increase your understanding of your
own thought process.

The same type of exercise may be done orally with a
partner. If you are working with another person, ask your
partner to simply repeat the word for you, allowing you to
give your associations between repetitions. If you are silent
for a few moments, your partner should simply repeat the
word, pausing long enough between repetitions to allow
you as much time as you want to give your association.
After five or ten minutes, depending on how long you
want to work, switch roles and repeat the word for your
partner. Individuals differ widely in their responses to this
word, though it is familiar to everyone. You may find that
you and your partner differ a great deal, or you may have
many associations in common. The person who speaks
first has some advantage, starting with a clean slate. The

person who speaks second will have to allow for all the
words he or she just heard, but will no doubt have fresh
associations to add.

Once you have worked on verbal associations for some
time (you will know intuitively how long is long enough
for you), you may want to work on eliciting imagistic associations. Instructions for eliciting imagery are given in
other chapters, but for purposes of continuing to discover
your associations you can simply close your eyes and visualize an image that for you would symbolize intuition.
One person saw a chalice, another a crystal ball, another a
triangle of light. You may get something in a flash, or you
may not. If you do, you may want to draw it or make a
note of it. If you do not get anything, don't be discouraged. Chapter 4 will provide further directions for
developing awareness of inner imagery.

Receptivity

In addition to relaxation and concentration, the process
of awakening intuition requires receptivity to all forms of
subjective experience. A noninterfering alert awareness,
maintained in the midst of the inner world of sensations,
emotions, and ideas, is the key to expanding intuition. Ultimately intuitive knowing transcends distinctions between
subject and object, knower and known. The process of
awakening this non-dual awareness, however, involves *disi-
dentifying* from internal states and observing them. This
disidentification of the observer self from the body, feelings, and ideas is sometimes called awakening the inner
witness. Roberto Assagioli refers to disidentification as the
means whereby a person learns to discriminate between
the contents of consciousness and its center. The center of
pure awareness or "I" he defines as a center of will, capable of mastering, directing, and using all physical and psychological processes.[6] Self-observation or self-awareness
thus implies the possibility of self-mastery and the voluntary control of internal states. Active attempts to simply
exert control, however, do not achieve the desired results.

First one must learn to observe without interference, maintaining an attitude of letting be, accepting whatever is going on without judging it or trying to change it.

RECEPTIVITY TO FEELINGS

Awareness of both the contents of consciousness and of yourself as the *context* in which they occur, aids the process of disidentification. Being identified with a particular emotional state, for example, is often fraught with anxiety and fear of being overwhelmed. Once disidentified, one has the freedom to express feelings whenever one chooses. Letting go of attachment to specific feelings also allows one to be more present in the moment and to give full attention to a person, problem, or situation as it presents itself.

Attending to feelings without changing them is even more difficult than attending to your breathing without changing it. Often, when you deliberately choose to get in touch with feelings, negative emotions such as anger or fear will come into awareness, and you may be tempted to shut them off or change them in some way, rather than allow them to be there. Keeping anger or fear below the threshold of consciousness by suppressing or repressing it, however, does not make it go away. Furthermore, repression takes energy, which is then unavailable for the task at hand, whether it be engagement in interpersonal relationships or concentration in any form. In practicing concentration, feelings often appear to be intrusive. By being receptive to them and allowing them to be there, you will not be diverting your energy and attention into trying to make them go away.

Feelings are often attached to something that happened in the past or something that might or might not happen in the future. Guilt, for example, is a feeling which is always attached to something one did or did not do in the past. In order to be fully present in the moment, free to give full attention to whatever you are doing, it is necessary to disengage yourself from past experiences. If you are plagued by feelings of guilt, you cannot see clearly what is happening now. The willingness to experience it fully, and to get in touch with any other emotions, such as resentment, anger, or fear that may be associated with it, can be a great relief.

Attachment to positive emotions can be just as distracting as avoidance of negative emotions. An intense experience of pleasure you would like to prolong or repeat will certainly detract from your capacity to be fully engaged in whatever is actually happening in the present. Think of your attention as a beam of light. When fully concentrated, it is coherent and powerful, like a laser beam. When diffused by emotional turmoil, attachment to the past, or anticipation of the future, it becomes incoherent or scattered, and loses its powerful intensity. Becoming conscious of what is intuitively known to you at any given moment depends on your capacity for noninterfering, concentrated attention on what you are aware of right now.

The most direct way of learning to focus attention and improve concentration, then, is not to *try* to let go of the emotional attachments that interfere with the process, but simply to observe them. Your feelings can give you important cues about what is appropriate for your further growth and development. Don't try to turn them off. Notice them, acknowledge them, experience them, just as they are. They too can be a channel for the expression of intuitive knowledge. Intuition on the emotional level can function fully only when you are aware of feelings, without judging them as good or bad, and without assuming that you have to act on them or do anything about them. There is no need to justify or rationalize a feeling.

Sometimes you might have a feeling about something you do not understand. Presentiments of danger, for example, may be inexplicable even in retrospect. One man in a workshop who was an experienced skier said he was able to avoid being caught in an avalanche on a cross-country skiing expedition by acting on apparently irrational feelings of apprehension. Another workshop participant related an incident in which he helped someone else out of a serious predicament by acting on what he thought were absurd feelings. He said he had been working on a construction site and, after he had already started home one evening, felt a completely inexplicable urge to return to the site. He did so, and found that one of the crew who had stayed late, alone on the job, had fallen and was hurt. He was able to get the assistance needed, and remarked that he probably saved the man's life.

Tuning in to feelings does not necessarily involve hunches or presentiments, although acting on feelings is part of learning to trust nonrational forms of perception. The decision whether to act on a feeling or not, however, is a secondary step which involves reason and choice. The first step, being receptive to them, is what contributes most to expanding awareness and developing intuition. Furthermore, in order to choose a path with a heart, or to live life whole-heartedly, you need to know how you feel. It is not possible to genuinely get into your work or be open to intimacy if you are out of touch with your feelings. Often feelings are repressed because they are painful. But when you repress painful feelings you inevitably repress other feelings, reducing your capacity for experience and closing off vital parts of yourself.

Opening up your awareness of feelings should not be confused with being overwhelmed by them or letting them run your life. It is one thing to be aware of feeling scared when trying out a new experience; it is something else to be immobilized by fear. Likewise, it is one thing to acknowledge being angry about something and then make a choice about whether or not to express it; it is something else to fly into an uncontrolled rage when something is upsetting. Once a feeling is experienced, you can begin to observe it with some detachment and disidentify from it. Assagioli has formulated the basic psychological principle as follows: "We are dominated by everything with which our self becomes identified. We can dominate and control everything from which we disidentify ourselves."[7] Thus you may be aware of *having* fear, for example, as part of the contents of consciousness, without becoming identified with it or controlled by it. Unlike repressed feelings, which distort perception, contribute to chronic tension, and distract one's attention from the present, emotions which are observed with detachment come and go and change naturally.

As you develop the capacity for an expanded awareness of feelings in which you try neither to hold on to positive emotions, nor to get rid of negative ones, you will realize that all emotions are transitory. Even deep depressions, which sometimes seem interminable, can and do change. Nor do highs last forever. Yet both are clearly part of the human experience, and to the degree that you are willing to expand your range of experience, you also expand your capacity for perceiving, understanding, and knowing more. It is the attachment to emotional states that interferes with the awakening of intuition, not the emotions themselves.

RECEPTIVITY TO IMAGES

Another aspect of expanding awareness of internal states without interference is the recognition and observation of inner imagery. While the use of imagery to encourage the development of intuition is covered in subsequent chapters, the focus here is on developing a greater awareness of the visions, daydreams, dreams, or fleeting hypnagogic impressions that appear spontaneously in the mind's eye. Everyone thinks in pictures before learning to think in words, and new insights and ideas frequently come in the form of images. Inner imagery also colors perception in ways that may not be immediately apparent. Thus, becoming conscious of the images and fantasies through which perceptions are filtered is a necessary part of developing the self-awareness on which clear intuition depends.

One of the most obvious ways in which images affect perception is through memories. Impressions in the present are often colored by memory images that may appear at the most unexpected moments. You have probably had the experience of meeting someone who reminds you of someone you knew at some other time in some other place. Sometimes the memory image is so strong that old feelings associated with the person you used to know lead to all sorts of unsupported assumptions about the new one. Becoming aware of how personal memories and associations distort and influence your perceptions helps clarify the difference between what is present experience and what is imagined or added to that experience.

The inner world of imagery reflects the outer world of experience, though often in distorted ways. Likewise, the outer world reflects the inner. Thus two people observing the same events may have very different perceptions of what is happening. Well-developed intuition is a clear and accurate perception of reality, both inner and outer. Intuition allows one to see into the nature of things, not by learning *about* them, but by identifying with them in such a way that subject/object boundaries dissolve. Self-awareness is the key here. To be at one with oneself, to perceive accurately what is true about oneself, is no small task. Yet this type of self-awareness is essential to freeing oneself from personal fantasies and projections.

Projection is the unconscious process whereby you see in another person something you do not wish to acknowledge or accept in yourself. Projections can be either positive or negative. Often when you admire someone you are projecting your own undeveloped potential onto that person, such that he or she appears to have all the virtues and assets you lack. For example, if you are an aspiring student of Buddhism, you are likely to project your own Buddha nature onto your teacher. Conversely, when you dislike someone, the person you dislike most probably has characteristics which you have repressed or disowned in yourself. A very assertive woman, for example, may hate sweet, submissive women, and vice versa. Sometimes projections are even more generalized and pervasive, as in the case of an angry person who sees the whole world as angry and hostile, and who may even deny that he or she is angry. The less willing one is to take responsibility for one's state of mind and acknowledge being its source, the more one's perception is subject to distortion by projection.

The topic of projection is relevant here because, ironically, it is closely related to intuition and often confused with it. Like intuition, projection operates by identification with, rather than information about, something or someone. However, projection is misperception, whereas intuition provides genuine insight.

Owning one's projections, in order to get them out of the way of intuition is, like owning one's emotions, a matter of disidentification and awakening the inner witness. Awakening the nonjudgmental inner witness does not mean splitting oneself into actor and observer, with some kind of dialogue or conflict going on between the two. The inner witness is, rather, an expanded consciousness of the *context* of experience.

The willingness to experience the intuitive process without evaluation or interference precedes the ability to do it. Learning to hold the ego in abeyance, to have it stand aside in order to get in touch with a deeper level of experience, takes practice in concentration, and a subtle, skillful exercise of the will. The paradox here is that while an effort of will is required to focus the mind and tune in to intuitive messages, the act is one of surrendering to experience rather than trying to shape it or control it. It is a process of learning to let things happen, rather than trying to make them happen. The only way to understand this paradox of learning to give up control in order to gain it, is to experience it subjectively. You can begin to learn about it by reading or talking to other people who have experienced it. But in order to *know* it, you must observe your own inner processes.

When you begin to observe your inner imagery and trust your subjectivity, you can easily feel the difference between the images which come to mind spontaneously, and deliberate vizualizations. People who have difficulty visualizing, imagining, or thinking in metaphors need to learn to let go of their tendency to control inner experience. Those who have no trouble in allowing the flow of imagery, on the other hand, need to learn to focus their attention in order to take responsibility for these experiences and not feel overwhelmed by them. The development of intuition depends on learning both control of the mind and surrender of the egotistical will.

The desire to maintain control over subjective experiences often stems from fear or anxiety aroused by the prospect of surrender. Practice in self-observation and awakening the detached inner witness can be helpful in overcoming resistance to exploring the deeper realms of intuitive knowledge. As Meher Baba said: "He who speculates from the shore about the ocean must be willing to plunge into it."[8] When one does plunge into the depths of one's own being, and directly experiences oneself as a center of pure consciousness, distinct from the contents defined by sensations, emotions, or thoughts, duality is transcended. There is, in pure awareness, no distinction between subject and object, observer and observed. This, then, is the foundation of intuition as the non-dual mode of knowing.

Ken Wilbur describes this paradox as it appears in the Chinese philosophy of Taoism: ". . . the authorization of all mental tendencies without interfering with any of them (*wu-wei*) would itself result in no-thought (*wu-nien*) . . . What Wei Wu Wei would have us do, therefore, is *dis-identify* ourselves from all phenomenal, perceptible, particular and *exclusive* objects, therein to discover our original and timeless unity with *all* manifestation."[9] Wilbur goes on to point out that this disidentification does not entail any particular action, but depends on understanding that what one can know, see, feel, or think is not the self, since all such perceptions are objects, inevitably separate from the self as subject. This split between subject and object is what Wilbur calls primary dualism, and it is precisely this duality which disappears in the intuitive mode of knowing.

One of the biggest obstacles to the development of this awareness is the desire for ego gratification. When motivation is predominantly geared to personal gain, intuitive insights are likely to be confused with either wishful thinking or neurotic anxiety. Some level of anxiety is, of course, normal and realistic whenever one is exploring the unknown, but when it becomes an obstacle to further growth and explorations it needs to be resolved and overcome.

When you begin to practice self-observation, therefore, it is useful to take stock of your motivations and the level of anxiety you experience when doing different exercises. Remember that self-deception is a formidable obstacle, so be honest with yourself when you consider your motives. Here again, observe without judging. You can only start from where you are, and since you are doing this for yourself and no one else, the more honest you are about what you are experiencing, the more rapidly you will learn to enjoy the creative resources of your intuition.

One basic exercise for developing self-awareness can be practiced in very brief intervals anywhere, at any time— whenever you are not *doing* something else. It is easier to start your practice in a situation where you can close your eyes for a few minutes and withdraw your attention from the external environment. This will give you the space you need to tune in to what is going on inside. Most people tend to give precedence to what is going on outside themselves as they go about their daily activities and interactions, attending to the body and emotions only when they hurt.

Self-Awareness Exercise

Begin this exercise by sitting quietly with your eyes closed. Be aware of any physical sensations which are present for you at this time. Notice the parts of your body that feel tense, and notice the parts of your body that feel relaxed. Check yourself out from head to toe, and be aware of those parts of your body that you were out of touch with when you began the process. Notice the parts of your body that move when you breathe. Notice where you are holding on. Be aware of your breathing without trying to change it. Is there any extra work going on in your body which you don't need right now? Let go of it now, or let it be. Pause. Be aware of any feelings that are present for you at this time. Notice any feelings pertaining to something that happened in the past, and any feelings pertaining to something that might or might not happen in the future. There is nothing you have to do about those feelings now. Just notice them, and let them be. Pause. Notice any thoughts that are going through your mind at this time, without trying to hold on to them, and without trying to push them away. Just notice them, and let them be. Pause. Notice any images that may be present in your mind's eye. Don't try to change them or hold on to them, just let them be. Be aware of sensations, feelings, thoughts, and images that are present, and notice how it feels to be you at this moment. Pause. Stay with your inner awareness as long as you wish. A few minutes is all that is necessary at first. Later on you may wish to prolong it.

Once you have learned to tune in to your inner awareness of the physical, emotional, and mental levels of your experience, you can do so quickly and easily. This does not mean practice and effort can be avoided. In fact, when you begin to realize that this practice enables you to be more fully conscious in everything you do, you may wish to expand it to include formal, disciplined methods of insight meditation. Joseph Goldstein, a teacher of insight meditation, writes: "Intuitions come out of the silent mind; imagination is conceptual. There's a vast difference. That's why the development of insight does not come from thinking about things, it comes from the development of a silence of mind in which a clear vision, a clear seeing, can happen. The whole progress of insight, the whole development of understanding, comes at times when the mind is quiet."[10]

Summary

In summary, there are three basic steps in training the mind for optimal development of intuition. The first step is quieting the mind. Any form of meditative discipline will contribute to your ability to do this. Physical relaxation is associated with a quiet mind, thus training in relaxation is an important aspect of this part of the work. The second step is learning to focus attention, or concentrate on that aspect of reality that one chooses to contact at a particular time. The third step is the cultivation of a receptive, nonjudgmental attitude that allows intuition to come into conscious awareness without interference. You cannot *make* intuition happen, but following the three steps outlined above prepares you to receive and acknowledge it when it does.

Individual responses to such training vary a great deal, but the development of nonjudgmental self-awareness and its effect on intuition is often associated with improved self-esteem and a sense of inner direction. Learning to trust intuition seems to be intrinsically satisfying when you are willing to learn by trial and error. Intuitive experiences are characteristically associated with increased or new awareness. Often experiences are intense and total, involving the whole of one's being. Individuals reporting such experiences often refer to a sense of being guided or directed by something other than reason. Such experiences are frequently unexpected and yet are almost always marked by a clarity of vision and a feeling that the experience is "right" or appropriate at that particular time. Spontaneous intuitive experiences can and do occur when a person is active either physically or mentally, but in training oneself to be receptive to these intuitive insights, the receptive process outlined above is the best way to begin.

Review Exercise

Take a few minutes now to quiet your mind, relax, tune in to your present awareness of sensations, feelings, and thoughts, then reflect for about five or ten minutes on your own life and your own experience of intuition. How does intuition operate in your life? What experiences have you had that you would consider intuitive? What type of intuition is most readily available to you? What type of intuition would you particularly like to develop further? Reflect on how you have treated your intuitive abilities up to this point in your life. How important do you think intuition has been for you up to now? Remember to maintain a nonjudgmental, conscious awareness of whatever comes into your mind in response to these questions.

No doubt intuition is already working in your life. Maybe not as much as you would like, but you have to start from where you are, not from where you would like to be. To find out where you are, write down answers to some of the questions above. Consider the intuitive experiences that come to mind as a result of the exercise. Your experiences will, of course, be unique. As you examine them, your intuition itself will emerge more clearly into your conscious awareness.

When you tune in to your intuition you also discover what you need for your own personal growth and development. There is no pattern that fits everybody. Some people need to work on developing concentration; others need to learn to let go. Some people need to get in touch with their feelings and to own them; others need to disidentify from them. You know better than anyone else what is going on inside you, but if you are out of touch with your own subjectivity, you are likely to feel confused and anxious about making choices and decisions which will affect your life. The more uncertain you feel, the more you need to justify, rationalize, and explain your views. On the other hand, the more conscious you are of how intuition operates and how your beliefs shape your reality, the more easily you can take responsibility for your life and make choices which are intrinsically satisfying.

Begin now. How does it feel to be you at this moment? What is true for you right now?

2

Choosing Your Own Way

Knowledge has three degrees—opinion, science, and illumination. The means or instrument of the first is sense; of the second, dialectic; of the third, intuition. This last is absolute knowledge founded on the identity of the mind knowing with the object known.

—PLOTINUS

By now you have probably made a choice regarding this book. Having read thus far, you have chosen either to take the time to work on awakening intuition as you read, or not. Either way, it is useful to be aware of how your choices shape your experience.

Consider the choice factor in everyday life. Everyone makes hundreds of choices every day, both consciously and unconsciously. But choice is something you have to be aware of if you are really going to exercise it. It becomes real when you believe in it, when you recognize it and exercise it. The same is true for intuition. It becomes real and works for you when you are consciously aware of it. When it remains unconscious, it functions at the level of instinct. As you become more conscious, you become capable of tuning in to it and acting on it, and in acting on it, it becomes an effective factor in your life. Choice does not exist for you if you do not see that you have it. It is only when you see that there are many possibilities in any situation and many possible reactions that you can consciously choose what you really want. When you react to situations automatically, out of habit or conditioning, you do not experience yourself as free. Like choice, freedom becomes real only when you believe in it, when you know you have it. Very few people are physically restricted, and yet at times you may not feel free, seeing limitations rather than possibilities. Intuition allows you to see and to sense possibilities that are inherent in a situation but have not yet been realized. Thus it opens the way to inner freedom, which can then be expressed in personal choices and decisive action.

There are many levels of choice and many types of choices, both material and emotional. You can choose things you want, a place to live, a career, relationships, friends, and ways to spend leisure time. While it is easy to see that one has a choice in how to spend free time, sometimes one forgets that the commitment to the activity called work was also a choice. Some choices, like choosing a career or a spouse, can be made for a lifetime.

Choices are also made about levels of awareness. If you choose to change your attitude about something, your experience will change even when circumstances have not changed. If you choose to believe in your own freedom, you can exercise that freedom. If you choose to believe that you are the pawn of fate, the victim of circumstances, or the product of early conditioning, your experience will support that belief. What you choose to believe shapes your reality, and beliefs are invariably chosen intuitively. Rational decisions about beliefs are rare; generally, rational faculties are used to rationalize beliefs.

If you are willing to become more conscious of your own beliefs and the alternatives you are intuitively aware of, you can begin to see that to a great extent your life as it is now is the result of choices you made in the past, and that your future will evolve according to the choices you are making now. Every day you are creating your own subjective reality. Every day offers many opportunities for choice. You can choose to be open or secretive, to shirk or take responsibility, to experience anger and let it go or to hold on to it and harbor resentment, to keep or change your habits, to risk a new experience or stick to the familiar, to move toward someone or away, to risk intimacy or distance yourself from others. Making choices for your own growth, trusting your intuition, can become a habit. Each time you choose to take advantage of a new opportunity, trusting your intuitive sense of what is best for you, you are strengthening this habit, and the choices become easier and clearer. As your choices become increasingly self-determined and well-defined, you can have as much freedom as you choose to believe in.

The task at the moment is to become more conscious of the choices you are making now, since they will determine your future. Right now, for example, you can choose whether you want to give your energy and attention to developing intuition. You can choose the attitude with which you read this book. You can choose whether to take time to do the exercises. You can choose whether to be honest with yourself about what you really want. Right now you can choose whether or not to do the following exercise. Don't worry about whether you should or shouldn't do it. Rather, before reading the instructions, make an intuitive decision. Ask yourself: "Is it worth doing?" "Am I willing to devote some time to personal problem solving right now?" If the answer is yes,

> Close your eyes and allow your body to relax. Review in detail the last twenty-four hours of your life, giving particular attention to the choices you made during this time. Is there anything you would like to have done differently? Are you satisfied with the results of your choices? Did you pay attention to your intuition

in making these choices? Instead of judging your choices in terms of right and wrong, consider whether you liked the results. Were you satisfied with the choices you made and the way you made them? What alternatives were open to you?

Another exercise which is useful for increasing awareness of choices available is the following:

Make a list of all the *shoulds* you can find in your mind. Everyone has some beliefs about *shoulds* hanging on even when one has consciously tried to acknowledge them as choices. Try digging a bit, to see what *shoulds* are running your life. Perhaps you will find something like: "I should be more honest," "I should be more loving," "I should be working on my latest project," "I should quit smoking," or any number of other *shoulds*. Write them all down or tell someone about them. Make the list as long as you possibly can. When you have finished, go back to the beginning of the list and rewrite it or resay it, but change the wording so that each one becomes, "I could . . . but I have a choice." For example, "I should be more honest" would change to "I could be more honest, but I have a choice." "I should be more loving" would be "I could be more loving, but I have a choice." Review your list carefully and consider each item and the feelings that change when you shift from thinking of it in terms of *should* to thinking of it in terms of *could*, and having a choice.

This exercise is particularly useful when you are wrestling with some big decision or problem which seems to be fraught with conflicting *shoulds*. For example, "I should spend more time with my children" may conflict with, "I should be working and earning more money." Another example came to my attention recently when an unmarried woman friend of mine became pregnant at age thirty-five.

Circumstances were such that she was faced with the choice of having an abortion or having the baby and raising it by herself. She realized that she had been yearning to have a child for many years and had unconsciously wanted to get pregnant. For her the choice could not be made in terms of what she *should* do. From one point of view she should have the baby, from another point of view she should not. Regardless of the judgments others might make, she clearly felt that her choice was her personal responsibility, and she was free to go either way. She could find as many reasons to justify having the baby as she could to justify an abortion. What she chose is not relevant here, but in taking full responsibility for choosing freely rather than feeling compelled to go either way, she was subsequently satisfied that she had made the best choice.

Taking the time to tune in to your intuition and the most basic level of making the choices of everyday life is good practice for learning to use it as a reliable source of guidance in major decisions. Alternatives are always available, even when you do not see them clearly. Intuition can open up new possibilities, sometimes by allowing you to see alternatives you have overlooked, sometimes by offering a fresh, creative solution to a situation in which you feel stuck. Being a nonlinear mode of knowing, intuition can frequently point the way out of a double bind. Giving yourself the space to playfully consider alternatives as real options which could become available, despite rational objections, is a form of brainstorming. Letting all the possible and impossible alternatives into one's awareness can stimulate the creative process, which is so easily stifled by restricting awareness to a narrow range of alternatives bounded by preconceptions that perpetuate unsatisfactory patterns of behavior. Learning to play with opposites is the first step toward reconciling and transcending them. Intuition is thus a key to unlocking your creative potential in everyday life.

Playing the Game

Many of the exercises presented in subsequent chapters will be most useful if you maintain a playful attitude while exploring how they can work for you. Taking oneself and one's problems too seriously often interferes with receptivity to fresh, creative possibilities. Working with imagery for example, as the language of intuition, can be both an entertaining pastime and a powerful means of insight and self-knowledge that can take many forms.

For the moment, try playing a game with me. Could you tell me what you are like by using a metaphor? For example, what sort of book would you be? One friend of mine sees herself as a dusty leather-bound Victorian novel. Another fancies himself as a racy paperback. Sometimes I feel like a book of contemporary poetry. What type of book would represent how you feel about yourself at this moment? Learning to describe yourself in terms of metaphors can help you recognize how eloquent the language of imagery can be. Playing this game in a group where each person described others as the cars they appeared to resemble, my friend Jacqueline Larcombe was stunned by what she felt was an amazingly accurate description of herself offered by a twelve-year-old girl she had just met:

"I see you as a dusty-brown Mercedes sedan, four doors, maybe a few dents, definitely not new. You know, it doesn't look so good, but it's got a great motor!"

Sometimes it is interesting to check out your perceptions about yourself with the way others see you. One young man who wanted to be a sleek white Jaguar discovered that others saw him as a Land Rover. My daughter, who sometimes feels like a Porsche, remarked the other day that she was feeling like a beat-up VW bug. The language of imagery can often convey both feeling and insight much more directly than verbal explanations. Thus imagery serves as an excellent vehicle for conveying intuitive insights which may be difficult to communicate in words.

Anyone can play this game, and of course you can choose, if you prefer, to play it by yourself, or with whomever you want. Learning to play simply means giving yourself the option of using this way to learn more about your intuition. If you limit yourself to casual playing, however, you may find that your interest in intuition remains relatively superficial. It can be fun, but you may also want to explore in greater depth the various ways intuition can expand your life. This game can be played on many levels, but in order to play well it is necessary to know the rules and assumptions underlying the various forms the game can take. For instance, one needs to know, first of all, what intuition is. Let us turn to some definitions of intuition and examine some common assumptions about how it operates.

What Is Intuition?

Intuition is true by definition. If a seemingly intuitive insight turns out to be wrong, it did not spring from intuition, but from self-deception or wishful thinking. Intuition is defined in Webster's as "The power of knowing, or knowledge obtained, without recourse to inference or reasoning; innate or instinctive knowledge; familiarly, a quick or ready apprehension." Psychologists have made sporadic attempts to explain intuitive knowing in terms of subliminal perception, suggesting that intuition is simply being aware of things which had been perceived below the threshold of conscious perception.[1] Eric Berne, for example, defined intuition as knowledge based on experience and acquired through sensory contact with the subject.[2] If this were so, anything attributed to intuitive knowing could be accounted for if we had better memories, or more complete recollection of data acquired through the usual sensory channels. This type of explanation assumes that individual consciousness comes into the world as a blank slate and learns everything from experience of the environment. It also assumes that it is not possible to know anything which does not come into consciousness through the five sensory channels of sight, sound, touch, taste, and smell.

While this theory does account for many instances of intuition defined as knowing without being able to explain how we know, it does not account for them all. Many people report psychic experiences and precognitive dreams in which they are able to see or hear events which are taking place in some other place or at some other time. The literature on psychical research is full of anecdotes recounting instances of clairvoyance and precognition which cannot be explained in terms of subliminal perception. The fact remains that it is apparently possible to get information and know things intuitively by means other than the usual sensory channels. Numerous theories attempt to explain the phenomena of telepathy, clairvoyance, and precognition, but no single theory has yet provided an explanation satisfactory to the skeptical rationalist. Current research in parapsychology is focusing more on the question of how such phenomena occur, having accepted the fact that increasing numbers of people are developing psychic abilities. Indeed, many believe that everyone has the potential for psychic experiences and that these experiences represent a type of intuitive knowing which cannot be explained in terms of ordinary sensory input.

To some extent, intuition as a way of knowing still defies rational explanation, although investigators continue to search for clues as to how it operates. Nonetheless, we do know something about how intuition can be developed and trained. The primary concern of this chapter is to define intuition and to give you some perspective on what can result from its awakening.

Attempts to measure individual differences in intuitive thinking in the laboratory are reviewed by Malcolm Westcott in his book *Toward a Contemporary Psychology of Intuition*. In a laboratory situation, subjects differed in the amount of explicit information they required before attempting solutions to problems and in the degree of success they had in reaching solutions. These two characteristics were independent of each other (i.e., success was not related to the amount of information). Those individuals who were highly successful on the basis of less information than is usually required to arrive at an accurate conclusion were designated as intuitive problem solvers, while those who showed a propensity for acting on little information with poor results were called wild guessers. Two other categories of subjects were designated as cautious careful problem solvers (those who demanded a great deal of information and were successful in using it), and cautious careful failures (those who demanded excessive information and characteristically failed to use it adequately). Westcott noted that the successful intuitive thinkers tended to have slightly higher mathematical aptitudes than the other groups, but that the difference was small. Their verbal aptitudes and academic grades were not distinctive. However, certain characteristic attitudes differentiated them from the other subjects. According to Westcott, "They tend to be unconventional and comfortable in their unconventionality. They are confident and self-sufficient, and do not base their identities on membership in social groups . . . Their investments appear to be primarily in abstract issues . . . [and] they explore uncertainties and entertain doubts far more than the other groups do, and they live with these doubts and uncertainties without fear. They enjoy taking risks, and are willing to expose themselves to criticism and challenge . . . They describe themselves as independent, foresighted, confident, and spontaneous."[3]

Carl Jung has defined intuition as one of four basic psychological functions, the other three being thinking, feeling, and sensation. He characterizes intuition as the function that explores the unknown, and senses possibilities and implications which may not be readily apparent.[4] Intuition perceives what is hidden, and thus enables one to perceive obscure meanings in symbolic imagery, or subconscious motives in oneself and in others. It is also associated with insight, or the ability to understand the dynamics of a personality or situation. Jung distinguished between the introverted intuitive person, whose intuition focuses primarily on the inner world of the psyche, and the extroverted intuitive, whose perceptions of the external world consistently lead to frontiers of exploration. Many successful entrepreneurs who have an uncanny ability to know what will happen next in their businesses are of the latter type.

Intuition is also the psychological function operative in scientific inventions or discoveries. Mathematicians, for instance, readily acknowledge the value of intuition in formulating new hypotheses, and exercise proof and verification as secondary processes. Likewise in physics and other sciences, it is intuition which provides researchers with new possibilities to pursue with the instruments of science. The history of science shows clearly that great breakthroughs in human understanding have been the result of intuitive perceptions that are only later tested and verified.[5]

As any creative person knows, when one gives the imagination free rein, it is likely to produce a lot of worthless material along with that which is highly prized by the individual and/or society. What is characteristically intuitive in this process is the factor of inspiration. Artists know that the muse must be wooed. Creative inspiration cannot be commanded, yet when it comes it carries with it the tremendous power and energy which may enable the artist to achieve a truly great work. It also carries the conviction and certainty characteristic of intuitive insight. The artist may not be able to explain why he or she feels compelled to carry out a particular piece of work, but he or she knows it must be done. The intuitive faculty leads the artist into new ways of expression and, whatever the medium, serves as the link between the individual and the universal experience given expression in a work of art. Thus, the source of true art is always an intuitive cognition of reality.

Philosophers concerned with universal truth and epistemology have regarded intuition as a way of knowing in which the separation of subject and object is transcended. The knower becomes one with the known, and knows from inside, by identification with, rather than information about, what is known. The word *intuition* comes from latin *in-tuire*, which can be translated as looking, regarding, or knowing from within. As a way of knowing, it is experiential and holistic. When one knows something intuitively, one knows it for sure, although one may not be able to explain the feeling of certainty. Intuition is true in the same way that sensation is true: it is your experience, and you know it for what it is. In this sense intuition is much more than a hunch or vague feeling. It may at times come into awareness only marginally, and seem vague, but if given attention, it can become increasingly clear and useful.

In Western philosophy intuition has traditionally been associated with direct apprehension of absolute truth. For Bergson, intuition is primarily an experiential event. It is through intuition that one may attain direct contact with prime reality. For Spinoza, intuition provides a superior way of knowing ultimate truth without the use of either prior knowledge or reason, although intuition of any great importance is likely to occur only after the full use of reason. Intuition and reason are considered entirely different processes which yield different kinds of knowledge. Only intuition is inevitably accurate, and only intuition yields knowledge of ultimate reality.[6]

In Eastern philosophy intuition is considered a faculty of mind which develops in the course of spiritual growth. Sri Aurobindo describes intuitive knowledge as "a lightning flashed from the silence and all is there, not higher or deeper, in truth, but just there, under our very eyes, awaiting our becoming a little clear—It is not so much a matter of raising oneself as of clearing obstructions."[7] In the course of evolution, humanity may be expected to tran-

scend the present mental level and become more and
more intuitive.

In the Tibetan Buddhist tradition, Lama Govinda
defines intuitive mind as being simultaneously one with
universal mind and with differentiated knowledge. It is
through intuition that the essence of life may be apprehended.[8] Another Tibetan teacher, Chogyam Trungpa,
teaches that in the intuitive mind we find that all is
within us.[9]

In Buddhism reason is seen as limited, and the knowledge derived from it is transient and unreliable. Reason is
therefore not considered a trustworthy source of knowledge of the absolute reality underlying a change. The
Buddha taught that intuition, not reason, is the source of
ultimate truth and wisdom. In Zen meditation, the discriminating conscious mind is quieted, and the intuitive
mind is liberated. In the experience of enlightenment the
individual returns to the true self or original nature, which
is void, and yet contains everything. The student of Buddhism is advised to look into his own mind to find out
what is true. The original Buddha nature inherent in all
living things is also the true nature of the self; therefore,
discovery of one's own true nature is the way to enlightenment or liberation.[10] Since the true nature of the self is
no-thing, self-discovery and self-transcendence become
identical.

The philosophical perspective on intuition is currently
being investigated in transpersonal psychology. Recent
psychological and physiological research has indicated significant differences in the functioning of the right and
left hemispheres of the brain. The left hemisphere is associated with rational, logical, linear thinking, and is characteristically verbal, while the right hemisphere is associated with intuitive, holistic pattern perception, and is
characteristically nonverbal. The kind of thinking which is
attributed to the right hemisphere is sometimes called
metaphoric thinking, and is frequently conveyed in images
and various artistic forms of expression. As a result of

these findings, many educators are becoming interested in learning how to educate the intuitive functions, which have been too long ignored in traditional education. The benefits of educating both sides of the brain, the intuitive *and* rational, are now widely acknowledged. Those whose formal schooling gave them no opportunity to cultivate intuition are finding ways of developing their intuitive abilities in other contexts.

Robert Ornstein, research psychologist at Langley Porter Neuropsychiatric Institute and professor at the University of California Medical Center in San Francisco, contends that while Western thought is left-hemisphere dominated, oriented toward rational, verbal, linear thinking, Eastern thought is primarily influenced by the intuitive, nonlinear mode attributed to the right hemisphere. He also points out that these two modes of knowing are complementary to one another; neither is reducible to the other.[11]

Western psychology has traditionally viewed as normal the rational linear view of reality which perceives the world as a multiplicity of separate objects and organisms, and experiences life as a sequence of events in time. This view of reality posits a duality of subject and object, and a split between spirit and matter. It is based on a mechanistic Newtonian model of physics which is now outdated. Contemporary subatomic physics, on the other hand, suggests a picture of reality that is much closer to the Eastern mystical view of reality, as an interdependent, interrelated unity wherein everything is in a continual state of change and transformation. Fritjof Capra, a physicist at the University of California in Berkeley, tells us that the universe of the modern physicist, like that of the Eastern mystic, is a system of dynamic, interacting, ever-moving components of which the observer is an integral part. He says,

> The basic oneness of the universe is not only the central characteristic of the mystical experience, but is also one of the most important revelations of modern physics. It becomes apparent at the atomic level and manifests itself more

and more as one penetrates deeper into matter, down into the realm of subatomic particles.[12]

Lawrence LeShan, a research psychologist in New York, has also discussed the similarity of world view between mystics and physicists, and points out that this view is shared by clairvoyants. After many years of thorough investigation of paranormal phenomena, he says: "Behind all the paranormal and the mystical lies the knowledge of the essential unity of man, with his fellows and the rest of the cosmos. This basic unity is reflected again—behind the screen of the mathematics—in Einsteinian physics."[13]

Capra suggests that what is needed is not a synthesis but a dynamic interplay between mystical intuition and scientific analysis. LeShan sees each of these two ways of comprehending reality as appropriate for different things. He says, "The deepest goal is to integrate the two in our lives, so that each viewpoint is heightened and sharpened by the knowledge of the other."[14]

These two modes of knowing may also be designated as two different levels of consciousness, namely the personal and the transpersonal. Transpersonal means beyond the personal. Western psychology has, in the past, viewed as normal the ordinary waking state of consciousness in which personal consciousness predominates. At this level the world is perceived as a multiplicity of objects and events, existing separately in time and space. Transpersonal consciousness, in which the underlying oneness of the universe comes into awareness and the ordinary confines of time and space are experientially transcended, has commonly been dismissed as delusional or hallucinatory experience. Eastern mysticism, on the other hand, asserts that true reality is essentially one, or non-dualistic, and that all distinctions and separations are illusory. Thus personal consciousness has been rejected as illusory in the East, and transpersonal consciousness similarly rejected in the West. In fact, both these levels of consciousness are part of human experience, and both are necessary for the fulfillment of human potential. Different cultures and different forms of mental training favor one or the other. Human beings have the capacity for experiencing directly both of these aspects of reality. Reason, which works through differentiation and distinction, is the mode of knowing appropriate to the personal level. The transpersonal level, beyond duality, can only be apprehended intuitively. In turn, direct experience of the transpersonal level affirms and evokes the intuitive mode of knowing. The task at hand is not to reject either of these views in favor of the other, but to expand our understanding and experience of consciousness to include both.

Whatever you choose to believe about the nature of reality and the role of intuition in your life, be aware that the choice is yours, and inevitably affects your experience. Once accepted, beliefs and values have a powerful influence on both subjective experience and behavior. Roger Sperry, noted brain researcher at the California Institute of Technology, writes: "A substantially altered picture of causal determinism in behavior is now inferred in which all subjective mental phenomena, including subjective values, are recognized to have a causal role per se in the decision-making process, rather than being mere correlates or aspects of a self-sufficient brain physiology. In any decision to act, the conscious mental phenomena override and supersede the component physiological and biochemical determinants. Even subjective feelings about projected outcomes anticipated to result from a given choice as far as 25 or 100 years in the future may be entered proactively as causal determinants in the cerebral operations that lead to a given choice."[15]

The implications of consciously choosing beliefs go far beyond personal experience. Priorities in goal setting on every level of human endeavor are determined by beliefs about the nature of reality and what is possible and desirable for human beings. On a personal level, whatever choices you make inevitably affect the lives of others. In choosing to share the process of awakening intuition, for example, you may make it easier for others to do the same.

3

Varieties of Intuitive Experience

> This term [intuition] does not denote something contrary to reason, but something outside the province of reason.
>
> C. G. JUNG: *Psychological Types*

Having defined intuition as a mode of knowing and a psychological function which is potentially available to everyone, let us turn our attention to examining the variety of human experiences which are commonly called intuitive. Intuitive experiences include, but are by no means limited to, mystical insights into the nature of reality. Experiences which are commonly called intuitive also include discovery and invention in science, inspiration in art, creative problem solving, perception of patterns and possibilities, extrasensory perception, clairvoyance, telepathy, precognition, retrocognition, feelings of attraction and aversion, picking up "vibes," knowing or perceiving through the body rather than the rational mind, hunches, and premonitions.

Intuition is often associated with having a hunch or a strong feeling of knowing what is going to happen. Often these hunches are vague, and since they are rarely recorded they are seldom verifiable. In conducting workshops and seminars on intuition I have often asked people to talk about whatever intuitive experiences they may have had, before defining or explaining the term. The most common response is of having experienced some instance of a hunch or premonition coming true. Do you remember a time in your own experience when you felt you knew something was going to happen, even though you had no reason for knowing it, and it did? For example, many people say that they sometimes know who is calling on the telephone before they answer, although there is no logical way of determining who it is.

One example of inexplicable hunches which turned out to be accurate was the story of a young woman who had planned a honeymoon trip to Tahiti several years ago. Shortly before the date set for her wedding, she dreamed of an airplane crash. She had such a strong presentiment that the plane she expected to fly on would crash that she canceled the reservations and changed her plans. The airplane she would have taken did crash, and everyone on board was killed. Another woman in one of my groups told us that for years she had harbored an irrational fear that her youngest daughter would be run over. She had two older children, about whom she had never felt this worry. One day, when her daughter was thirteen years old, she was hit by a car and taken to the hospital for emergency treatment of head injuries. The girl was not seriously hurt, and recovered quickly. The mother said she felt a tremendous sense of relief, and has not been bothered by that anxiety since the accident. She felt as though she had been expecting it to happen, and had been dreading it, but now she did not have to worry about it any more.

Does having a strong hunch or presentiment allow one to do something to alter the course of events? The answer seems to be yes, as in the case of the young woman above, although it is not always clear what can be done. Some people are afraid of their hunches and would prefer not to notice them. Unfortunately, however, repression does not eliminate fear. If you are a person who is plagued by irrational fears and inclined to have pessimistic hunches which rarely come true, it would be advisable for you to examine your fears. Psychotherapy can help to overcome such fears, and by increasing self-knowledge it can also help in learning to distinguish fearful presentiments from intuition.

At times hunches may seem negative, such as the hunch that you will forget something when you go on a trip. At other times they may be positive, such as the hunch that you will get a job you applied for even though the competition is stiff, or the hunch that you will do well in an exam despite inadequate preparation. What is necessary in the beginning, regardless of whether the hunch is positive, negative, or neutral, is to learn to distinguish genuinely intuitive hunches from those which are simply a product of anxiety or wishful thinking.

The best way to do this is to keep a record of your hunches in a journal or a diary. In this way you can check up on yourself, to see how often your hunches turn out to be accurate. Subjectively you may begin to notice that intuitive hunches feel different from those which turn out to be purely imaginary. The only way you can learn to make the distinction for yourself is to learn by trial and error. At first, when you begin to keep a record of your hunches, you may find a high percentage of errors. As your sensitivity to nonverbal cues, both internal and external, is refined, your record may improve. Don't be discouraged by errors. Every time you make an error you have the opportunity to learn something about yourself. If you are willing to acknowledge yourself as the source of your error—that is, to take responsibility for it rather than blaming it on outside circumstances—you may quickly learn to see how your personal interests distort your perceptions and get in the way of clear intuition.

The conscious mind, or ego, frequently interferes with intuitive perception. The more you want something to happen, the less you are able to sense whether it will happen or not. For example, if you want someone you love to call you, you may think it is him or her every time the phone rings, only to be disappointed each time. On the other hand, someone you hardly know, or whom you have not thought about in weeks, may come into your mind inexplicably, and then, a few minutes later, that person may call. Fear and desire both interfere with intuitive perception. If you are anxious, angry, or emotionally upset, you are not likely to be receptive to the subtle messages which can come into consciousness via intuition.

At the same time, strong emotional ties between people often seem to facilitate telepathic communication. In the overwhelming majority of cases of spontaneous dream telepathy recorded by England's Society for Psychical Research, the sender and the receiver (i.e., the dreamer) were related to each other or were friends. The most common themes were death, danger, and distress. A mother, for example, dreamed of her son calling out to her when he was dying overseas, and later received the report that this actually happened.[1] During the Vietnam War, in the late 1960s, when I was leading dream groups in connection with my work as a psychotherapist, I personally heard of several instances of mothers dreaming of their sons being wounded or killed in battle either when it occurred or before they heard the news. A teen-ager in one of my groups recounted a vivid and disturbing dream of her father's death in an automobile accident, which she had the same night that it happened although he was in another state and she knew nothing about his life at the time.

The experimental research of Montague Ullman and Stanley Krippner at the Dream Laboratory of Maimonides Medical Center in New York provides convincing evidence of telepathy, clairvoyance, and precognition in dreams. Drs. Ullman and Krippner report that regardless of profession, walk of life, waking psychic ability, or knowledge of having ever before experienced ESP (extrasensory perception), the great majority of subjects described correspondences that were "suggestively telepathic." The authors attribute the success of their experiments in dream telepathy over waking telepathy, established by quantitative testing, to the use of potent, vivid, emotionally impressive human interest pictures to which both sender and receiver can relate. They also suggest that successful activation of ESP may be related to a relaxed, passive state of mind.[2]

Telepathic messages do not always come in dreams. A woman in one of my intuition workshops shared her experience of feeling a wave of strong emotion one afternoon while having coffee with a friend. Her strong feelings of apprehension seemed to be a mixture of fear and sadness related to her mother. After a short time, when the feelings did not subside, she called her mother, who was in another city. She learned that her mother had suffered a heart attack at the moment when she had first been aware of the feelings, and was in a critical condition. Her apprehensive feelings had been so painful that she felt relief rather than shock when she heard the news.

Charles Tart, professor of psychology at the University of California at Davis, who has conducted extensive research on ESP, asserts that ESP is one of the most complex psychological processes. The information apparently flows in unknown quantities into the unconscious mind and is subject to all sorts of alterations and distortions because of the receiving subject's belief systems, psychological needs, and unconscious dynamics. One method for determining the effects of belief on performance in ESP described by Dr. Tart was to divide subjects into "believers" and "disbelievers" and analyze their ESP scores separately. For this purpose subjects were asked to indicate their degree of belief in whether they could exercise ESP in the testing situation, before being given the test. Dr. Tart reports that believers consistently tend to score above chance, whereas disbelievers score significantly below chance expectation.[3]

Lack of acceptance of intuition in the culture at large

certainly contributes to its suppression in individuals who do not want to be "different." Many adults in my groups have said that they felt they were more intuitive as children, and that they learned to keep their intuitive perceptions to themselves after encountering skepticism or ridicule from adults. One woman who attended an intuition workshop recalled an incident in her life when she was about five years old. On a Friday she announced to her mother that Grandmother would not be coming to dinner on Sunday because she had hurt her foot. Her mother did not pay much attention to her remark, as she assumed she was making it up. To her amazement, the following day Grandmother called and said she would not come to dinner the next day because she had sprained her ankle the previous afternoon.

Such incidents may be frightening to adults who do not understand them or consider them paranormal. Parents who are afraid of what seems incomprehensible often respond angrily to intuitive observations by their children. They may attempt to explain them away, or to deny the child's experience, saying something like, "You couldn't possibly know that. Don't lie to me." At best, the child's remarks may be ignored.

Frances Wickes writes that a very intuitive child is often difficult for parents to handle. She describes the typically intuitive child as one whose rational thought processes are largely unconscious. "He frequently seems to grasp the situation by a sort of magic contact and so gives back the desired response, but how he arrived at his conclusions is a mystery even to himself. He just 'knows it is so.' Sometimes, because he cannot retrace his steps and supply the missing logic, he is accused of willful guessing in an attempt to assume knowledge which is not his, but this is as unfair an estimate of him as to accept his answer as a proof of his powers of logical thought."[4]

Young children learn very quickly that there are some things they are not supposed to talk about. For many this reticence persists into adulthood. Participants in intuition workshops often express appreciation for having the opportunity to talk about experiences which they would ordinarily not discuss for fear of being considered "weird" or "crazy." Children seldom share their inner world of fantasy and perception with adults, because sympathetic, understanding adults are rare. Although it is socially acceptable for a preschooler to indulge in fantasy play, when a child goes to school he or she is bombarded with external stimuli designed to teach him or her to live in the reality of the external world. Although children and adolescents often have a very active intuition, since it is unimpeded by other functions,[5] it is seldom dealt with in education. At school the inner world, where intuition is nourished, is usually closed. A child whose natural intuitive abilities are strong enough to survive social censure may develop into an exceptionally creative person, but what about all those whose talents simply remain repressed or undeveloped?

Most people fall into the second category. They are trained in school to use rational and intellectual abilities as well as they can. Individualized instruction attempts to allow each child to learn at his or her own rate, but even this learning is primarily geared to the acquisition of information from external sources. Little attention is given to the inner world. Even the advent of affective education, which takes into consideration a child's emotional development along with his or her cognitive development, does not include the development and training of intuition. Thus, as adults, many people feel a need to redress the balance, and learn to follow the promptings of their own psyche.

In general, intuition flourishes only when it is valued, and clearly certain lifestyles and experiences facilitate or nourish it. Inspiration needs space and attention if it is to take shape in a creative endeavor. Attention acts as psychic energy and enhances the process it values. The artist who is highly intuitive in his or her perceptions of reality knows that inspiration always seems to come of its own accord. Effort is invariably involved in the creative process, but flashes of inspiration tend to occur spontaneously. Seeking inspiration requires a receptive mode of consciousness, and is comparable to trying to remember something you know but have forgotten. Tarthang Tulku, a Tibetan Lama, writes: "If we wish to regain some memory or insight that is 'there,' but is temporarily elusive, it is often most effective to put aside any grasping or tight achievement-orientation and become passively receptive. By quietly opening the mind, the hidden element is allowed to present itself on its own. In a similar manner, artists seeking inspiration used to go to sleep, hoping for a visit from a muse, who would speak to them—and then through them—in their art. People courting divine intercession have long understood that they must *open* themselves to divine messages and purposes, as in the cases of prayer and oracles. According to all these various orientations, the importance of surrendering the self has been emphasized."[6]

In a sense, everyone is an artist in charge of designing his or her life. If the unexamined life is not worth living, what about the uninspired life? Certainly many, if not most, people in our society would not consider their lives to be particularly inspired. Yet the possibility is there for *everyone* to tap the creative source of inspiration which comes from well-developed intuition.

The kind of intuitive experience which leads most directly to a sense of well-being and harmony with oneself and the universe is the mystical or transpersonal experience. The mystical experience is characteristically described as one in which the individual transcends the subject/object dichotomy, feeling him- or herself to be at one with everything. In this experience there is no separation between inner and outer, knower and known. It is sometimes described as the experience of pure consciousness, with no specific content. Various levels of mystical experience are described in both Eastern and Western mystical traditions. Stanislav Grof has defined transpersonal experiences as those involving "an expansion or extension of consciousness beyond the usual ego boundaries and beyond the limitations of time and/or space."[7] What these experiences have in common, and what concerns us here, is a universal affirmation of the human capacity for transcending ego boundaries and the limitations of the rational mind, and the fact that the essential truth of reality can only be apprehended intuitively. It is this direct apprehension of truth which characterizes pure, spiritual intuition.

This type of intuitive experience is often fleeting, yet it can have a profound effect on a person's life, for an experience of cosmic consciousness dispels all doubts and answers all questions, and replaces them with feelings of bliss, awe, wonder and joy.[8] The individual who is open to this type of intuitive knowledge experiences a sense of unity or oneness with all things, and a sense of illumination or enlightenment. What was formerly hidden becomes clear, but not necessarily once and for all. Such an experience of enlightenment can continue to deepen and expand in the process of living, or it can be denied and repressed.

In contrast to the sudden, spontaneous flashes of pure intuition which occur with no particular preparation, the systematic development of intuition is one of the aims of yoga. In yoga true intuition is considered a stable, reliable function of the higher levels of consciousness from which a wide range of information is accessible. Techniques of meditation provide the means through which one may discover and develop this type of awareness.[9]

Remember that intuition of spiritual truth is something you already have inside you. As you discover who you are and become more familiar with the transpersonal dimensions of your experience, you will become increasingly conscious of it. This kind of truth is recognized, not learned. For most people the process of learning to look within to find their truth requires spending some time clearing away the confusion that distorts clear awareness. But as this process is learned, personal benefit can result from the steps involved. The way itself is also the goal, as every step has intrinsic value and provides satisfaction.

Levels of Intuitive Awareness

The broad range of intuitive human experiences falls into four distinct levels of awareness: physical, emotional, mental, and spiritual.[10] Although any given experience may have elements of more than one level, experiences are usually easy to categorize according to the level at which they are consciously perceived. For example, mystical experiences are intuitive experiences at the spiritual level, and as such they do not depend on sensory, emotional, or mental cues for their validity. Intuition at the physical level is associated with bodily sensations, at the emotional level with feelings, and at the mental level with images and ideas.

Physical Level

The intuitive experiences defined as inspirational or psychic frequently depend on physical and emotional cues that bring them to conscious awareness. At the physical level a strong body response may be experienced in a situation where there is no reason to think that anything unusual is going on. The kind of jungle awareness which enables primitive people to sense danger when there are no sensory cues of its presence, is a highly developed form of intuition at the physical level. It differs from instinct in that instinct remains unconscious, while intuition becomes fully conscious, although a person may act on it without stopping to justify or rationalize it. The person simply knows something he or she needs to know without knowing how he or she knows it.

For people living in an urban environment this type of awareness is no less useful. Though it may not always be particularly dramatic, it can also be a matter of life and death. When you are in a situation that is uncomfortable for you, you may notice such bodily symptoms as tension, headaches, or stomachaches. If you stop to pay attention to these cues, you may find that you are indeed in a situation which is unhealthy and which is creating undue stress on the organism. If, for example, you always get a stomachache when you attend staff meetings at work, you should probably consider what needs to be changed in the situation to reduce the stress, even if this means a change in jobs. If you pay attention to physical symptoms which on the surface seem inexplicable, you may very well find out a lot about what your needs are. The cues of intuition on a physical level are not, however, always easy to perceive. Unfortunately, one often fails to acknowledge messages from the body until they become painful. If you are attuned to your body, you will notice your body responding differently to different people and different situations even without a stomachache or a headache. At times you may feel open, warm, and responsive, and at other times you may feel that you want to close up and withdraw. Learning to trust your bodily responses is part of learning to trust your intuition.

Bodily responses are a source of information about both yourself and your environment. Ann Dreyfuss, a Reichian therapist in San Francisco and professor of psychology at the California State College at Sonoma, reminds us that the body is one's access to the world. "It is possible," says Dr. Dreyfuss, "to be out of touch with oneself, unaware of one's body and in conflict with one's bodily process. Such disharmony distorts one's view of the world, one's perceptions and conceptions. A basic way of working toward personal enrichment involves increasing congruence between body and awareness . . . Whatever dimension of the outer world one considers, it is through the body that one experiences it, and it is through the body that one distorts it to make it comprehensible."[11]

Noticing physical symptoms of stress can often allow you to take care of your physical and emotional needs before they reach a painful or destructive level. Intuitive insight into your personal needs cannot only prevent serious disorders, but can also give you a direct indication of immediate needs. The desire to close up and withdraw, for example, may be an indication that the situation is not appropriate for you to open up in, or it may indicate an inner need for stillness and solitude. Or, if it is a habitual response, it may be related to some underlying fear which is preventing you from expanding your life and exploring new possibilities. If this is the case, you may want to change the pattern, and the first step is to become aware of what is happening to you. When you become aware of your body responses, you can choose whether or not you wish to act on them. Sometimes you may experience tension in response to a particular situation and choose to leave. Other times you may experience tension and choose to remain and confront the difficulty. Either way, being conscious of body responses is an essential part of a holistic intuitive awareness of yourself in relation to your environment.

Research indicates that one responds physiologically to events in the environment even when such responses remain below the threshold of consciousness. In an experiment carried out by Charles Tart at the University of California, a subject sitting in a darkened, soundproof chamber was asked to tap a telegraph key when he thought he received a "subliminal stimulus." He was not given any stimulus, but in another soundproof chamber several rooms away a "sender" received an electric shock at random intervals. The sender attempted to send a telepathic message to the subject each time he received a shock to make him react and tap the key. This attempt proved unsuccessful; the key taps were unrelated to the sender's messages. Bodily responses, however, *were* related. Brainwave and heart-rate measurements indicated that the subject was responding physiologically to the telepathic stimulus, although he was not conscious of it.[12]

Dr. Tart's work suggests that one *can* be influenced by extrasensory stimuli even when one is not aware of it. The task of awakening intuition at the physical level, then, is inextricably linked to increasing awareness of what the body already "knows."

Emotional Level

On the emotional level, as on the physical level, awakening intuition is inseparable from developing self-awareness. On this level intuition comes into consciousness through feelings. Sensitivity to other people's "vibes" or "vibrations of energy," instances of immediate liking or disliking with no apparent justification, or a vague sense that one is inexplicably supposed to do something, can be instances of intuition operating on this level.

When you learn to tune in to your feelings, they can become just as clear as bodily sensations in giving you information about a particular situation, be it a matter of changing jobs, finding a partner, or merely deciding what to do on a free weekend. How you feel about yourself, your relationships, and everything you do is related to how willing you are to take emotional intuitive cues into account when you are making choices. The better you know yourself, the more you can trust your intuition when it attracts you to someone you would like to know better, or warns you not to get involved. Occurrences of love at first sight, although they can be explained away as projection, may also be strongly intuitive. A woman in one of my classes described meeting her husband in a group five years ago. She said she knew the minute she saw him that he was *it* for her, despite the fact that "He didn't look like much," and she did not feel a strong physical attraction for him at first. Less romantic, but nonetheless meaningful instances of intuition at the emotional level occur every day.

What is commonly called "woman's intuition" is intuition on the emotional level. There is no evidence that men and women are inherently different in their intuitive capacities, but the popular belief that women are more intuitive than men is related to the fact that women in our society are not taught to repress feelings as much as men. Little boys are taught early not to cry and not to be emotional. Little girls may escape some of the rigorous training in rational intellectual development, which is stressed for boys wanting to be successful in a highly competitive society. Boys, however, are just as capable as girls when it comes to developing the intuitive functions of the right hemisphere of the brain.

Judith Hall, Assistant Professor of Psychology at Johns Hopkins University, Baltimore, reports that research in the area of sensitivity to nonverbal communication indicates that women tend to be more attentive to visual cues such as facial expression, body gestures, tone of voice, and the way people look at each other or touch each other. Females do score higher than males in tests designed to measure accuracy of interpretation of nonverbal communication. There is, however, no data to support the belief that these differences are inherent. On the contrary, one study cited by Dr. Hall showed that more traditional males scored lower at nonverbal judging than more liberal males, and more traditional females scored higher than more liberal females. The differences reported by Dr. Hall are not large, and she points out that these findings suggest that eliminating strong gender roles could make male and female scores converge.[13]

Although this type of perceptual awareness contributes to one's understanding of other people, it should not be confused with developing awareness of one's own internal feeling states. Intuition cannot be reduced to observation of behavior, body language, and other visual cues. It is a holistic awareness which includes both internal and external sensitivity, and which sometimes transcends sensory input altogether.

At the emotional level, women and men who are aware of their feelings and who follow them tend to be comfortable with their diffuse intuitive understanding, except when called upon to give a logical, rational justification for actions based on intuitive feelings. Demands for explanations, either from oneself or from another, are usually met with inadequate rationalizations that fail to satisfy anybody. Rarely is someone willing to say simply that he or she chose to do something simply because it felt right. Nevertheless, people in all kinds of occupations and lifestyles do act on the basis of intuitive feelings, and feel that their decisions are better for it.

Expanding awareness of the emotional level of intuition is often associated with an increase in synchronicity and psychic experiences. For example, you might feel like calling someone with whom you have not spoken in some time for no particular reason. If you act on the feeling, you may discover that the person you called had been trying to get in touch with you, or that it was timely for you to call just then. You may discover later a reason for your intuitive feeling, or you may not. However, the more you act on your feelings and take the risk of checking out the validity of your intuition, the more reliable it can become.

Sometimes intuition on this level will tell you something about your interpersonal relations that you would rather not know, and in these instances it may seem easier to repress it than to act on it. You might, for instance, meet someone you think you would like to befriend, although you have a feeling that this will not happen. When I was in graduate school a friend of mine had told me how much he wanted to get to know one of our professors whom he greatly admired. One night he dreamed that he was talking to him, but the professor did not say much, and refused to take off his overcoat. As my friend reflected on what the dream was telling him, he realized that he had felt intuitively that this man had wanted to keep his distance ever since they met. Repeated attempts to get better acquainted were of no avail. He later regretted the time and effort expended, for he had "known" all along that it would be fruitless.

Recognizing and valuing what is true for you at a feeling level does not necessarily involve other people. A shift in mood, a change in perception, may also be experienced as an awakening of intuition. Elizabeth Herron, a contemporary poet, writes about her experience with this type of awakening, noting the difficulties of communicating verbally about this subjectively meaningful experience:

> I was depressed. The world had gone flat and colorless. I had withdrawn. I was a tiny kernel inside my body, adrift amid necessities and obligations, oppressed by my separateness, cut off from the wellsprings of my soul. I walked up to the pond, took off my clothes and plunged into the water —a sudden shock, cold against my skin. Floating to the surface, I heard a bird call across the meadow. Suddenly, I was at the stillpoint. The bird's call was my voice. We were separate and yet one. I was out there and in here. . . . All things converged in me and radiated from me. "The center of the circle is everywhere, the circumference nowhere." I recognized this, knowing it had always been so, though I had been cut off from my experience of it. My head filled with poetic images. The dimension of the infinite was everywhere.
>
> This was a repetition of similar experiences. It is a paradoxical awareness. In these moments I KNOW. But my knowing is not enough. I must struggle to comprehend what I know. My intuitive knowledge must be expressed in order to be communicated. I cannot share my experience merely by telling you about it. As a poet, I seek words for my experience, but words alone are not enough. There are realities—nuances of feeling and meaning, for which words are inadequate.[14]

Artistic endeavor in all its forms often provides a way of expression for this type of intuitive awareness. But it is not necessary to be an artist to benefit from conscious sensitivity to feelings. Emotional states invariably color perceptions of reality as well as provide information about one's relation to others and the environment. Perceiving the world through feelings is like wearing a pair of colored glasses which can increase acuity of vision yet color everything with a particular hue. Recognizing that one is wearing colored glasses (i.e., acknowledging that perceptions are distorted by emotional states) is part of learning to distinguish intuition from personal emotional reactions.

Mental Level

Intuition on the mental level often comes into awareness through images, or what is called "inner vision." Patterns of order may be perceived where everything at first appears chaotic, or patterns of change may be apprehended intuitively long before the verification process of careful observation is completed. In the West, the intuitive flashes which follow the exhaustive use of logic and reason tend to be more highly valued than other types of intuition, since they are associated with the kind of discovery and invention involved in technological progress.

Intuition on the mental level is operative in the formulation of new theories and hypotheses in any field, for this type of intuition implies an ability to reach accurate conclusions on the basis of limited information. Although all intuition is mental in the sense that it is a function of the mind, intuition on the mental level refers particularly to those aspects of intuition related to thinking. Thus intuition on this level is often associated with problem solving, mathematics, and scientific inquiry.

Malcolm Westcott reviews the writing of mathematicians, with particular reference to Poincaré. Poincaré writes about the importance of intuition in his own work, and asserts that both intuitive and analytical activity are crucial to the advance of mathematics as well as the empirical sciences.[15] Jacques Hadamard confirms these views and adds the observations of other mathematicians. Hadamard quotes Einstein as follows: "The words or the language, as they are written or spoken, do not seem to play any role in my mechanism of thought. The psychical entities which seem to serve as elements in thought are certain signs and more or less clear images which can be 'voluntarily' reproduced and combined."[16] Einstein believed that objective physical reality can only be grasped by an intuitive leap, not directly empirically or logically.[17] He further asserts that the axiomatic basis of theoretical physics cannot be an inference from experience, but is a free invention of the human mind.[18] Writing on "The Structure of Creativity in Physics," Siegfried Muller-Markus supports this contention and concludes: "An idea like Planck's quantum of action was not logically entailed by experiment, nor could it be derived from previous theories. Planck conceived it out of his own self."[19]

The role of intuition in creativity and problem solving has also been recognized by individuals concerned with business management. Successful businessmen are typically intuitive on a mental level. Research indicates that successful executives tend to score far above average on ESP tests.[20] The ability to know intuitively what will succeed in any type of business certainly contributes to the success which is often attributed to luck. Henry Mintzberg suggests that managers should have well-developed right-hemispheric processes. It is important for managers to "see the big picture," says Mintzberg, and this implies a relational, holistic use of information (i.e., synthesis rather than analysis of data). He also points out the dearth of literature on this subject: ". . . despite an extensive literature on analytical decision making, virtually nothing is written about decision making under pressure. These activities remain outside the realm of management science, inside the realm of intuition and experience." Mintzberg supports the hypothesis that the important policy-level processes required to manage an organization rely to a considerable extent on the faculties identified with the brain's right hemisphere, and suggests that while policy makers conceive strategy in holistic terms, the rest of the bureaucratic hierarchy implements the policy in a linear sequence. Mintzberg points out that all intuitive thinking must be translated into linear order if it is to be articulated and put to use, and that truly outstanding managers are the ones who couple effective right-hemispheric processes with effective processes of the left.[21]

Although lateralization of brain functions may be overemphasized,[22] the basic point that intuitive thinking plays a vital part in decision making is supported by other authors in the field. Ostrander, Schroeder, Dean and Mihalasky maintain that people who have highly developed intuition are more successful. ESP seems to be particularly useful in decision making, economic forecasting, and personnel selection.[23]

Intuition in business is often referred to as a "gut feeling," yet a person whose intuition may be well-developed on a mental level is not necessarily one who is equally well-developed on an emotional level. Carson Jeffries, a physicist who attended one of my seminars at the University of California in Berkeley, told me that he valued his intuition and used it in his research, but felt out of touch with it in interpersonal relationships. For him intuition was working on the mental level, but not on the emotional level. After becoming aware of this he was able to expand the range of his intuitive ability to encompass more of his experience.

You do not have to be a scientist or a business executive to appreciate the value of intuition at the mental level. The sudden recognition of a pattern in your life, the "aha!" experience in psychotherapy when unconscious processes are suddenly illuminated, or the "eureka" of a new discovery, are ways in which anyone can experience this type of intuition. Such insights are often accompanied by mental imagery, but not necessarily. Pattern recognition is not always visual. It may be auditory to a musician, or simply a flash of understanding in which events or ideas seem to fall into place.

Melvin Calvin, Nobel Laureate in Chemistry in 1961, for example, describes his most exciting moment in research like this:

> One day I was waiting in my car while my wife was on an errand. I had had for some months some basic information from the laboratory which was incompatible with everything which, up until then, I knew about the photosynthetic proc-

ess. I was waiting, sitting at the wheel, most likely parked in
the red zone, when the recognition of the missing com-
pound occurred. It occurred just like that—quite suddenly—
and suddenly, also, in a matter of seconds, the cyclic character of the path of carbon became apparent to me, not in the
detail which ultimately was elucidated, but the original recognition of phosphoglyceric acid, and how it got there, and
how the acceptor might be regenerated, all occurred in a
matter of 30 seconds.[24]

Perhaps you have had the experience of struggling with
a problem or a decision until you were sick of it, and then
deciding to forget it for a while. Very often the solution
pops into your head when you least expect it. The expression "sleep on it" refers to allowing this intuitive process
to be completed during sleep. Many people report finding
solutions to apparently insoluble dilemmas through their
dreams and daydreams. When you stop trying to make
something happen, intuition is allowed to operate.

In their biofeedback research at the Menninger Foundation in Kansas, Elmer and Alyce Green have used the
term *passive volition* to describe the detached effortless volition required for the voluntary control of physiological
functions regulated by the autonomic nervous system.[25]
While active volition is necessary for the control of the
voluntary nervous system, passive volition is necessary for
the control of the so-called involuntary nervous system
which regulates such physiological functions as heart rate,
blood flow, and muscle tension. Subjects trained to increase or decrease the volume of blood flow in the hands
at will, for example, learn to do so through visualization.
As the subjects become aware of the subtle physiological
changes taking place, they learn to let them happen. The
Greens say: "Few people realize, however, that [the] feeling or intuition of freedom has unusual significance in respect to the autonomic nervous system."[26] In other words,
knowing that you can do something to affect a process
that you assumed was involuntary makes it easier to learn
how to do it.

Intuition at all levels is often experienced as arising spontaneously, and any attempts at voluntary control may at first appear futile. Once you realize however, that there are some things that you can do to allow it to emerge, it can be expanded voluntarily, and the rate of expansion can be accelerated.

Spiritual Intuition

Spiritual intuition is associated with mystical experience, and at this level intuition is "pure." Pure, spiritual intuition is distinguished from other forms by its independence from sensations, feelings, and thoughts. In a discussion of intuition in spiritual psychosynthesis, Assagioli considers intuition as an independent psychological function which is "synthetic" in that it apprehends the totality of a given situation or psychological reality. Assagioli says: "Only intuition gives true psychological understanding both of oneself and others."[27] In its purest manifestation, Assagioli maintains, intuition is devoid of feeling, and as a normal function of the human psyche, it can be activated simply by eliminating the various obstacles to its unfolding. At this level intuition does not depend on sensing, feeling, or thinking. It is not associated with the body, the emotions, or pattern perception relating to specific problems or situations. Paradoxically, the cues on which intuition depends on other levels are regarded as interference on this level. However, an awareness of how intuition functions on other levels helps to dispel the misconception that intuition as a way of knowing is an all-or-nothing proposition. Degrees of intuitive awareness may also be affected by such factors as time, place, mood, attitude, state of consciousness, and many other variables.

In Spinoza's terms, spiritual intuition is knowledge of God. James Bugenthal equates this knowledge with man's experience of his own being and says: "Man knows God in his deepest intuitions about his own nature."[28] Dr. Bugenthal describes the inward vision through which man discovers his nature as a creative process that does more

than observe what is already at hand, bringing into being
fresh possibilities.

Among those fresh possibilities is the potential for transcending duality and personal separateness. The capacity
for transcending duality is not particularly unusual. Abraham Maslow, in his study of self-actualizing persons in the
1960s, found that, "While this transcendence of dichotomy can be seen as a usual thing in self-actualizing persons, it can also be seen in most of the rest of us in our
most acute moments of integration within the self and between self and the world. In the highest love between man
and woman, or parent and child, as the person reaches the
ultimates of strength, self-esteem, or individuality, so also
does he simultaneously merge with the other, lose self-
consciousness and more or less transcend the self and
selfishness. The same can happen in the creative moment,
in the profound aesthetic experience, in the insight experience . . . and others which I have generalized as peak
experiences."29

Spiritual intuition as a holistic perception of reality
transcends rational, dualistic ways of knowing and gives
the individual a direct transpersonal experience of the underlying oneness of life. Describing the difference between
dual (rational, conceptual) and non-dual (intuitive, holistic) modes of knowing, Ken Wilbur writes: "If we are to
know Reality in its fullness and wholeness, if we are to
stop eluding and escaping ourselves in the very act of trying to find ourselves, if we are to enter the concrete ac-
tuality of the territory and cease being confused by the
maps that invariably own their owners, then we will have
to relinquish the dualistic-symbolic mode of knowing that
rends the fabric of Reality in the very attempt to grasp it.
In a word, we will have to move from the dimness of twi-
light [dualistic] knowledge to the brilliance of daybreak
[intuitive] knowledge—*if we are to know Reality, it is
to the second mode of knowing that we must eventually
turn.* Enough it is now to know that we possess this

daybreak knowledge; more than enough it will be when at last we succeed in fully awakening it."[30]

In yoga spiritual intuition is called soul guidance,[31] and is said to emerge spontaneously when the mind is quiet. In writing about the teachings of Sri Aurobindo, Satprem describes the intuitive mind as follows: "The intuitive mind differs from the illumined mind by its clear transparency— . . . all is so rapid, flashing—terrible rapidities of the clearing of consciousness." Although intuitive knowledge may be translated or interpreted according to personal preoccupations, it is "always, essentially, a shock of identity, a meeting—one knows because one recognizes. Sri Aurobindo used to say that intuition is *a memory of the Truth*."[32]

The practice of meditation prepares the mind for the experience of spiritual intuition, by clearing away the obstacles which ordinarily interfere with its becoming conscious. Learning to recognize pure awareness or consciousness as the context of all experience, distinct from the contents of consciousness, is one way of understanding this level of intuition.

In order to make a subjective distinction between your own consciousness and its contents you can try the following experiment: Write down everything you are conscious of at this moment. Do this for several minutes. When you have done this, notice what you left out. At any given moment you are conscious of only a fraction of what is going on in your mind. Consciousness is selective, and the normal range of awareness is extremely narrow in the ordinary waking state. When consciousness begins to observe itself, however, it begins to expand. You may notice that while you are reading this you are simultaneously aware of your surroundings, what time it is (approximately), whether you are feeling hungry or thirsty, and you may also be wondering when your friend will call and how you are going to make arrangements for what you want to do tomorrow. You may also be reviewing an unsatisfactory conversation you had with someone earlier in the day. Can you observe your own stream of consciousness in a manner that is satisfactory to you? Or are there so many streams running simultaneously in all directions that you cannot observe them all? Learning to empty the mind in order to experience consciousness devoid of contents is one of the objectives of meditation. By observing your thoughts, feelings, and sensations without interfering with them, you may begin to experience that quiet state in which spiritual intuition unfolds.

Activating spiritual intuition means focusing on the transpersonal rather than the personal realms of intuition. At this level it is consciousness as context, rather than the content of consciousness, which comes into awareness. Other forms of intuition focused on sensation, feeling, and thinking become obstacles to pure awareness, empty of content. If you become too engrossed with the powers that intuition can make available to you at other levels, you may fail to recognize your potential for developing spiritual intuition. Yet this dimension of intuition is the basic ground from which all other forms of intuition are derived.

Intuition In Your Life

Intuition at any level will lead you into what is new or unknown. No matter what level you are working on or which way you think you are going, intuition leads you past the boundaries of what you once knew into areas of new discovery. No matter how much you know, there is always more to be discovered. Intuitive experiences, regardless of whether they occur spontaneously or as a result of training, invariably expand consciousness to include more of reality, and more understanding of what is true.

If you reflect on your life and consider the turning points which led you into new experiences, you may recognize the role of intuition. You cannot know in advance what the outcome of a particular course of action will be. Decisions are based on what *is* known, *and* on what is intuitively felt to be the right course. Few people get married, move to a new place, or take up a new career without some doubts and uncertainties about whether they have made the right decision. Such decisions may even appear to be irrational or at least semirational. A person may leave a secure job in order to explore a new career in a completely different field. Or a person may impulsively inquire about attending a workshop or class which is of little interest, and end up enrolled in something that profoundly influences his or her personal growth. One couple attending a workshop on intuition said they had intuitively chosen the town in which they live as the place they wanted to be, without knowing why. Now, ten years later, they know they made the right decision.

How many times have you chosen one course of action over another on the basis of intuition? Make a list of the spontaneously occurring instances in your life when you were aware of acting on your intuition. Take time to reflect on whether you made the right choice, and what alternatives were open to you. Ask yourself whether you can trust your intuition, and notice how it works for you in your life. A good way to develop intuition further is to talk to a friend about intuition and discuss your intuitive experiences. Many people who are quite aware of their intuition do not talk about it because they are concerned about appearing strange or unusual. Yet when people are invited to discuss their intuitive experiences in my workshops they enjoy talking about them. They also seem pleased and relieved when they find others who share their interest and like to talk about their own experiences with a sympathetic listener. It is often reassuring, if you have not discussed how intuition works in your life, to know that it is operative in everybody's life, in one way or another.

Spontaneously occurring intuitive experiences can offer a renewed sense of vitality, excitement, and engagement with life. Mystical or transpersonal experiences which have no material goal or purpose can totally transform one's view of reality. Intuition is involved not only in the practical decisions which shape your life, but also in your choice of beliefs about the nature of the universe. Belief systems are often chosen unconsciously and they can shape one's perception in such a way as to vitiate alternative beliefs. The term "belief system" does not refer strictly to religious beliefs, but to all assumptions about reality. Today widespread exposure to a variety of religious doctrines makes it possible to choose beliefs that seem true rather than remain for a lifetime within the bounds of religious dogma, but unconscious assumptions may be hard to recognize.

Everyone makes assumptions about the nature of reality, and these assumptions form subjective belief systems rather than objective observations. These belief systems may be attributed to early conditioning, but as soon as one is willing to question them and consider alternative views, one opens up the possibility of choice. What you believe to be true shapes your experience, and beliefs are chosen intuitively, not rationally. Lawrence LeShan defines a metaphysical system as a set of assumptions about how the universe is put together and how it functions. He suggests that the metaphysical system you are using is the metaphysical system that is operating.[33] If this is so—and Dr. LeShan has done extensive research to support this view—it is worthwhile to examine the belief system you have chosen to run your life. The process of expanding intuitive awareness means exploring, questioning, and perhaps changing some of the assumptions you have taken for granted up to now.

4

Imagery and Intuition

The greatest insight, thought and art concerning the human condition and its divine aspirations are rooted in the phenomenon of inner vision.

—José and Miriam Arguelles: *Mandala*

Imagery is the universal language of the unconscious. Thinking in pictures precedes thinking in words, and this type of primary thinking continues to be a part of subjective experience throughout life in the form of dreams, fantasies, and imagination. Imagery is a powerful tool for self-regulation and self-development, and can also be a vehicle for profound intuitive insights. Imagery is associated with direct perception, and conveys in an instant feelings and observations which would take many words to describe.

Learning to understand the language of imagery is just as necessary as learning to listen to bodily sensations and feelings in the process of expanding intuitive awareness. By paying attention to the body one discovers that one is capable of increasing sensitivity to physical and emotional experience. In attending to imagery, one finds that imagination has a great deal to do with determining emotional states. Imagery can be highly charged emotionally, even when it does not make sense to the rational mind. Inability to understand the meaning of a particular image that appears spontaneously in a fantasy or a dream does not diminish its emotional or physiological impact.

The physiological effects of imagery also make it a useful tool in biofeedback training. The Greens have found that migraine headaches can be successfully treated by training subjects to voluntarily raise the temperature in their hands and cool the forehead through visualization.[1] If you simply *try* to raise the temperature of your hands, probably nothing will happen. But if you visualize yourself standing in front of a fire warming your hands, or imagine that you are immersing your hands in warm water, the temperature may change quite quickly.

The Greens have formulated a psychophysiological principle as follows: "Every change in the physiological state is accompanied by an appropriate change in the mental-emotional state, conscious or unconscious, and conversely, every change in the mental-emotional state, conscious or unconscious, is accompanied by an appropriate change in the physiological state."[2] Thus the ability to control physiological processes through visualization affects mental-emotional states, and these in turn affect the awakening of intuition. The Greens point out that "the desired behavior is obtained through visualization of the desired event accompanied by volition."[3] They also indicate the desirability of learning to maintain a state of relaxed awareness, as in reverie: "Reverie is a state of unusual significance because with it is associated hypnagogic-like imagery in which unconscious processes are often revealed to the waking self in symbols, words, or Gestalts."[4] Hypnagogic images are characteristically vivid, original, changeful, and independent of conscious control. Wilson Van Dusen, writing about hypnagogic imagery, describes it as the antithesis of ego.[5] Where ego is absent, it appears, and learning to observe it means learning to lay aside ego.

Research on the effects of imagery implies that all mind-body processes may be voluntarily controlled. Furthermore, the Greens suggest that such training in internal awareness and control is expected to be highly significant in learning how to combine conscious and unconscious processes in the creative shaping of ideas. Like intuition, the creative process is never entirely volitional and involves both letting things happen and taking responsibility for shaping them.

A subjective distinction must be made between imagery which occurs spontaneously and imagery which is deliberately induced. Both are useful, but they are not the same. Deliberately induced imagery is used most frequently for bringing about physiological changes. You can experience this type of effect by trying the following exercise:

> Close your eyes and imagine that you are holding a lemon in your hand. Visualize the lemon as clearly as you can, and imagine feeling the texture of its skin with your fingers. How big is your lemon? Notice the bump on one end of it and the place where the stem was attached on the other end. Notice the little dots on the skin and the color. Now imagine that you put the lemon on a table, take a knife, and cut the lemon in half. When you have cut the lemon, notice whether it has a thick skin or a thin skin. Notice the different segments, the white parts and the greenish-yellow parts. Can you smell the oil from the skin? Notice any drops of lemon juice appearing on the cut surface. Imagine that you squeeze a few drops of lemon juice on your tongue and taste it.

You may find that simply reading this description of the exercise causes you to salivate. On the other hand, you may try the exercise with your eyes closed and still not experience the activation of the salivary glands consciously. Preceding the exercise with a period of relaxation and quieting the mind helps to make the imagery more vivid and the effects more noticeable. In any event, if you were able to detect any tendency to salivate when you focused your attention on imagining tasting the lemon juice, you now know, experientially, that imagery has a direct effect on a process which normally is involuntary.

Another way of experiencing the effects of imagery is through memory. If you think about someone you know, for example, you can remember what he or she looks like without going through a linear description of his or her physical appearance. When you think of a particular person, you not only recall what he or she looks like, you also have a feeling about the person which is present to some extent when you think of him or her. You need only to think of someone you like or dislike intensely, visualize him or her as clearly as you can, and notice whatever feeling responses and physical sensations are present for you when you do this in order to experience the direct effects of imagination on your physical and emotional state.

The emotional impact of imagery is also easily experienced by anyone who has felt strong emotions associated with dream images. In fact, dream images are frequently highly charged emotionally, and are therefore useful in psychotherapy as a way of getting in touch with suppressed feelings. Using dreams, fantasy, and imagination as tools for personal growth is called working with "affective imagery."

The ability to visualize may facilitate the process of working with affective imagery, but imagery is by no means limited to visual images. Although visual imagery is dominant for most people in this culture, many individuals are more responsive to auditory, kinesthetic, or olfactory images. Auditory imagery involves the imagination of sound. It may include music or words, but can also take stronger forms. For example, the emotional impact of roaring, screaming, buzzing, grating, etc. can sometimes be even more powerful than visual imagery, from which you can distance yourself as a spectator.

Olfactory imagery is particularly evocative for some people, but kinesthetic imagery, involving body movement, is probably the most completely involving form of imagery. Kinesthetic imagery which is fairly common includes the sensations of falling, swimming, flying, running, or other physical activity. This type of imagery is also suggested in relaxation exercises which call attention to feelings of heaviness, and hypnotic induction techniques which suggest a sensation of floating. Kinesthetic imagery associated with dance and body movement often evokes deep unconscious feelings both in sleep and in the waking state.

The impact of affective imagery on a person's life depends to a considerable extent on the degree of participation in the imagistic experience on a sensory, kinesthetic, affective, and conceptual level. It is the fullness of participation which gives this type of inner experience transformative power. When you do not participate but only observe your own symbolic imagery as if it were a filmstrip, it may seem a meaningless and insignificant curiosity. However, imagery is the language of the unconscious, and as such it serves as a vehicle for bringing unconscious material to consciousness and is therefore useful for expanding intuition and promoting psychological health.

Although the ability to disidentify from thoughts and emotions is appropriate at a certain stage of personal growth, and is essential to awakening the inner witness, in learning to work with inner imagery immersing yourself completely in the imagistic experience is appropriate and useful in the beginning. The more completely you identify with your inner experience, the deeper you will be able to penetrate into the creative wellsprings of your intuition. Disidentification is appropriate only after full identification. You cannot give up something you do not have. In other words, it is recommended that you own and experience your feelings consciously before attempting to transcend them. Letting go of anger, for example, is not the same as pretending it is not there. There is a crucial difference between self-transcendence and self-deception. Premature disidentification can lead to avoidance and escapism, whereas the willingness to experience fully whatever emotions are triggered by your imagery allows you to expand your experience and grow into a new level of awareness.

Increasing receptivity to imagery is a way of using imagination as a vehicle of intuitive insight. Imagery serves as the language of intuition, and the process of learning it is twofold: First one evokes inner imagery, then one interprets it. These two aspects should be clearly distinguished in order to avoid confusion. What you see in your mind's eye is one thing; what it means to you is another. Interpretation is a subtle secondary process which, in the initial stages of working with imagery, is apt to cause problems. Not only does it interfere with the spontaneous flow of imagery, but it can also lead to premature mistaken assumptions which contribute to self-deception rather than intuitive knowledge. For the moment we will focus on evoking the imagery, without interpretation.

A good way to begin is to visualize something fairly concrete, in which memory and imagination may easily be combined. The following exercise, for example, gives you an opportunity to exercise your imagination within a fairly structured setting.

> Imagine a house that you are about to enter. See what it looks like on the outside. Notice the entrance. Enter your house and explore the rooms. See what the furniture is like, and notice whether the windows and doors are open or closed. Go up to the attic and down to the basement. Are there any people in your house? What changes would you like to make in your house?

In response to these instructions a young woman recounted the following experience:

> The house I see looks like a small one-story cottage, covered with vines. I have never seen this particular house before. The area around the house is all overgrown. I notice some climbing roses. I enter to find the rooms much larger than I expected. The house feels pleasant and cheerful and sunlight

is coming in through the windows. Everything is a mess, and the furniture is old and crummy. The doors are open, but the windows are closed and dirty. The house needs cleaning and airing. The basement has a big furnace in it which heats the whole house. I also see some crates in the basement which I inherited from my parents. I don't want to look inside them, but I want to get rid of them and make the basement into a playroom. The attic is warm and quiet. It is dusty, with piles of books in it and a few pieces of old furniture. It is a cozy, comfortable place which offers an escape from the chaos in the rest of the house. There are no people in my house. The house needs to be cleaned out. I want to throw out a lot of the old stuff in it, wash the windows and fix it up.

In trying this particular visualization exercise, some people visit a house they have known rather than an imaginary house. Others create very realistic images, while a few individuals create fantasy structures which have no resemblance to the houses they live in. There is no right way to imagine a house. Whatever imagery emerges for you is what you have to work with. The more you are willing to accept whatever is there for you, the more quickly you will learn to trust your intuitive sense of what the meaning of it is for you. Interpretation of imagery is not a strictly rational, analytical function. It involves all your intuitive capabilities as well.

This particular woman had no difficulty recognizing the symbolic dimensions of her imaginary house and relating them to her view of herself. She knew that an imaginary house is sometimes interpreted as a symbol of the personality, and after reflecting on her fantasy, offered the following interpretation:

> The state of my house seems to reflect the state of my mind at this time. I feel that my head is cluttered with ideas, but I am reluctant to start the big job of housecleaning. That would probably mean therapy or analysis. I see the furnace in the basement as the energy of the unconscious, giving warmth and vitality to the whole house or personality. The

crates in the basement seem to symbolize unexplored elements in my unconscious, possibly introjected parental values. I don't want to examine them, but feel I must do so before I can get rid of them and make use of the basement for more creative activity. The attic represents a comfortable retreat into a world of books. It is not a place of active involvement. I need to throw out a lot of old, useless habit patterns if I want to be satisfied with myself. I would welcome other people in, but I am not ready to do so. My head is too cluttered for me to be genuinely available to other people. I feel I am ready to begin the task of putting my house in order.

Imagery cannot be meaningfully interpreted out of context. Your own imagery has meaning only in the context of your own life. Discovering what it means for you also provides an opportunity for self-discovery. This is one reason it is advisable to refrain from interpreting another person's imagery, since by doing so one deprives him or her of this opportunity of self-discovery. This process of self-discovery not only helps you to learn to use and trust your intuition, it can also give you insight into your own state of being. It is here that insight and imagination meet. Imagination is the means whereby insight is attained. Sudden insight, or the "aha!" experience, is characteristically intuitive. It is marked by a sense of knowing, or understanding, or seeing patterns and relationships and order where none appeared to exist before.

When you are trying to interpret your own imagery, remember that images always have both positive and negative aspects, and you, as the creator of the image, are the best interpreter of what it means in the context of your life. Others may help clarify something or offer their own associations, but the associations that are most important for you are your own. By gaining access to the meaning of your inner imagery you can begin to assimilate at least a part of the unconscious, thus expanding self-knowledge and integrating parts of yourself which were formerly unfamiliar, disowned, or projected.

Up to this point we have referred to inner imagery as a means of increasing self-knowledge. Inner imagery is also a source of inspiration, ideas, insight, and meaning. As you become accustomed to allowing your inner imagery to emerge spontaneously, the process tends to feel more like discovery than invention. At first you may feel that you are "just making it up." This may be an accurate observation, but it actually refers to the depth of the experience rather than to a specific technical difference. The images which are "just made up" are usually experienced as superficial and insignificant. Those which seem to emerge of their own accord and tend to resemble dream images take on added significance and meaning. The distinction is subtle but unmistakable if you have had the experience of eliciting both kinds.

The difference between images that are "made up" from images that "just appear" is also related to different modes of consciousness. Arthur Deikman, a psychiatrist in San Francisco, has pointed out a number of differences between the active mode which predominates in our daily activities, and the receptive mode which is cultivated in meditation.[6] The active mode is by no means limited to external activities. One may be very active internally even when sitting quite still in meditation, trying to control the mind in various ways. Even the effort to achieve a receptive attitude can be a form of activity. Thus when one is engaged in "making up" images, one is invariably active. When one is in the receptive mode, on the other hand, images may appear effortlessly, out of nowhere. To become familiar with the potentialities of inner imagery it is useful to do exercises that work with both modes. Here, however, the emphasis will be on expanding awareness in the receptive mode, since it is this mode which favors awakening intuition.

The receptive mode of consciousness is commonly experienced in states of reverie and during deep relaxation. Sometimes the emotional impact of imagery which emerges spontaneously in these states is evident even when the meaning is not. The personal significance of particular images may not be comprehended until much later, if at all. For example, Duane Elgin, a social scientist with well-developed psychic abilities, recalled recurrent images he experienced when growing up on a farm in Idaho. He intuitively recognized them as being significant although he did not understand them until much later, after he had undertaken some training in developing awareness. He wrote about his experience as follows:

> I was struck by the fact that visions I had as a child were enormously important. I am thinking of two in particular. From the time I was approximately four until nine years old there were two consistent, repetitive images that would appear with distinct clarity when I went to bed in the evening, well before going to sleep. It was not uncommon for these to appear at least several evenings a week, and during the course of any given night, they would alternate and repeat themselves three or four times before disappearing as I drifted off into sleep. These did not seem to be constructed images in that I had little control over their appearance and change of form. It was more like being a passive receiver which, when tuned in, could allow these images to manifest.
>
> Almost invariably, the first image would be that of grotesque black swirling forms of indescribable chaos and ugliness . . . repulsively ugly even though there was no "graspable" form . . . rather a literal essence of infinitely convoluted futility/frustration of black chaotic disorder . . . even with a nauseating sense of texture odor. It was like nameless, ugly, writhing black worms of chaos whose overall living image was quite distinct but no one element could be seen clearly and distinctly and, therefore, grasped. It remained always just out of the clutches of my concretizing/conceptualizing mind.
>
> Then a second vivid image, which was also quite distinct but ultimately ungraspable, would replace it: A point of bronze/gold/yellow/white light . . . without a visible center but with the obvious knowledge that its source contained a powerful but invisible energy . . . tremendously wise/warm/harmonious/comforting/radiant/gentle/soft/peaceful/infinite knowing. It had a clear source but

the source was not visible. It never had a clear point of origin although it was clear to me that its origin was in the center, the place of all reconciliation. It conveyed infinite peace, balance, and harmony. There was nothing but everything.

These two fluid images provided an important subconscious frame of reference from which I could test the world to see if my actions were contributing to chaos or balance in my own life. Perhaps the perception is now becoming more conscious. Although these images never had a clear form which could be held in my mind's eye and objectified, their character was unmistakably clear.

The state of consciousness that seems most conducive to the emergence of this type of imagery is deep relaxation, often on the threshold of sleep. Individuals who have experienced biofeedback training associate this state with the relatively slow alpha and theta brain-wave rhythms. The alpha wave, which indicates a brain-wave rhythm of eight to thirteen cycles per second, is associated with a state of relaxed, diffuse awareness. The slower theta wave is associated with the emergence of hypnagogic imagery, just before one drifts into sleep. The sleep state is registered as a delta brain-wave pattern. One woman with a well-developed capacity for imaging and clairvoyance said that the threshold between alpha and theta seemed most productive for her, since it was too easy to forget or lose images which appeared on the threshold of sleep.

When you begin to observe the flow of your own inner imagery, whether you give yourself a specific suggestion for visualization such as the exploration of a house, or simply begin to attend consciously to the spontaneous images which emerge when you are deeply relaxed, notice what form your imagery takes. Is it predominantly visual, auditory, or kinesthetic? Are you more aware of motion, form, color, texture, people, objects, or abstractions? Is your imagery flat, appearing as if it were projected on a screen or is it three-dimensional? Are you involved in the scene as a participant or are you simply an observer?

The emergence of this spontaneous imagery is commonly associated with right-hemisphere brain functions. Remember that the right hemisphere, thought to be predominantly intuitive, is considered nonrational and nonlinear in its functioning. In order to avoid interference and enhance your awareness of the intuitive right-hemisphere functions, it is best to quiet the rational analytical functions associated with the left brain hemisphere. As soon as you begin to control or manipulate your inner imagery, the logical linear thinking of the left brain is likely to reassert its dominance. Since the development of the intellectual, left-brain functions is stressed so strongly in our traditional educational system, the process of learning deliberately to put these functions aside, even if only for a short time, and replace them with more awareness of the intuitive functions, can be called *un*learning. Most people have been taught to process information critically —judging, evaluating, and discriminating in every facet of their lives. The process of developing a holistic intuitive awareness, however, necessarily involves a suspension of judgment and evaluation. This allows one to see what is there rather than what one thinks is supposed to be there. When it comes to interpreting what one sees or hears or feels in connection with inner imagery, the rational faculties are essential, but that is another process.

Increased awareness of the flow of inner imagery can also occur as a result of insight-oriented psychotherapy which explores the psyche in depth. Reflecting on his own experience in psychotherapy as a psychiatric resident, Roger Walsh made the following observation:

> One of the most wondrous discoveries [of therapy] was the slowly dawning awareness of the presence of a formerly subliminal, continuously changing stream of inner experience . . . Here was an ever-present, but formerly unsuspected veritable internal universe. After a couple of months I began to perceive more clearly a constant flux of visual images. One of the most exciting of many exciting memories is that of the sudden recognition that these images exquisitely

symbolized what I was feeling and experiencing in each moment. Here was a previously unsuspected gold mine of information about myself and the meaning of my experiences. As my sensitivity increased I found that the images accompanied subtle, physical sensations in my body, and that these sensations were the somatic representations of emotions . . . Experiencing this inner world began to become very pleasurable and whereas initially I had believed that my inner world must of necessity harbor unwholesome collections of monsters, which I had avoided confronting all my life, I now came to think of this inner world as a very attractive, pleasant source of positive information.[7]

The spontaneous flow of inner imagery can easily be stimulated by thinking about an abstract concept. The tendency to think in pictures is readily observable when you think about something like time. Close your eyes, relax, and allow yourself to be quiet for a few moments before trying the following exercise:

Think about a long time. Pause. Think about a very long time. Pause. Think about an even longer time. Pause. And longer. And longer still. Think about a time that is twice as long as that. And longer. Pause. And think about a time that is even longer. And longer. Pause. Think about eternity.

Almost invariably, when one is asked to think about an abstract concept such as a long time, some picture comes to mind. The variations are infinite, but in our culture most people have a linear concept of time, and images which emerge in response to the instructions given above often include a long, long road stretching off into the distance, flashes of historical scenes stretching off into the past, visions of geological changes in the earth, traveling out into space among the stars, and visions of future societies on earth. When you do the exercise, notice whether your vision of time stretched into the future or the past. Did you begin thinking in terms of minutes, hours, days,

weeks, years, or lifetimes? Where did you go from there?
Occasionally someone may think of time in terms of expanding the present moment. Since the present has no extension but intensity, a long moment may be experienced
as eternity immediately. Most people, however, spontaneously begin by thinking of a long time in terms of past
and future, and the emerging images reflect the in-
separability of time and space. When asked to think about
time, almost everyone visualizes it in terms of space.

Intuition itself is neither timebound nor spacebound.
Time and space do not affect intuitive perceptions of reality, yet the way in which one thinks about time affects the
ability to open up intuitive faculties. If one conceives of
time as linear, and believes it is possible to know the past,
but impossible to know the future, one is limiting oneself
according to what has been learned as "fact." Phenomena
such as clairvoyance, telepathy, and precognition are experienced by many individuals, and the fact that we do not
have a satisfactory scientific rational explanation for *how*
these phenomena occur does not justify pretending that
they do not exist. Psychic phenomena not only exist, but
are currently considered by increasing numbers of people
to be the next step in the evolution of human potential.
Science fiction has for some years been exploring through
fantasy the possibilities of expansion of psychic powers,
and when you begin to pay attention to your intuition you
will find that what you once considered strange, and perhaps a little weird, is perfectly ordinary, and within the
normal range of human potential. Knowing that something is going to happen before it happens, for example, is
not strange if you discard linear, spacebound notions of
time. Intuition is a way of knowing that transcends both
time and space.

Why should one be concerned with evoking images of
time and space if one is going to discard them? The main
reason—and in a way this is a matter of justifying the exercise to the questioning, rational mind—is that acknowledged preconceptions and limitations are easier to work

through than those remaining unconscious. Beliefs are limitations that must be transcended in order to break through to a new level of awareness, but one cannot see the limitations of beliefs unless one acknowledges underlying assumptions. Conceptualizing time as energy or in any other form is not our concern here. What is useful for the purpose of awakening intuition is to identify your own way of conceptualizing time, and recognize it as only one of many possibilities. The point is not to change your way of thinking, but to see that *any* way of thinking is necessarily limited. Whenever you define something, you limit it. Thus when you define intuition as a function which transcends time and space, you need to realize that it also operates *in* time. Indeed, intuition is often associated with seeing into the future, recognizing patterns and possibilities which are not readily apparent. In meditation the function of form is to carry the mind beyond form, and in working with intuition, thoughts, concepts, and imagination are the vehicles which carry awareness beyond themselves into the realm of pure intuition.

From this perspective let us examine some other ways in which inner imagery can be useful in learning to trust intuition. Throughout what follows remind yourself over and over again not to try to understand or interpret your images as they emerge, but rather simply to observe them. As soon as the discriminating, intellectual faculties begin to interpret the flow of imagery, the process itself is altered. Subjects who have been exceptionally successful in controlled telepathic experiments have noted that attempts to control the flow of images tends to interfere with accuracy. When a fleeting image is "brought back" it is already changed. Any attempt to make something happen, any active intention on the part of the subject, seems to interfere with the receptive mode of awareness which favors accurate perception in telepathic communication. Likewise, clairvoyance, or remote viewing, the ability to see and describe target locations and events at a distance, is also associated with receptivity to images which appear

to the subject with no apparent effort. Subjects who have
been successfully trained in controlled remote-viewing experiments confirm the importance of receptivity to images
emerging spontaneously in the mind's eye.[8]

Images of Interpersonal Intuition

The capacity to observe inner imagery in a receptive,
noninterfering way thus has the potential of yielding information not only about one's inner reality and subjective
emotional states—the aspect which is the primary focus in
working with imagery in psychotherapy—but also about
external reality. The question which arises at this point is
always, "How do I know if what I see is true?" "If I imagine that I see my husband/wife making love to someone
else, can I assume it is true, or does low self-esteem lead
me to conjure up fantasies which reflect my fears?" Such
questions cannot be answered out of context. The most
obvious way to find out if your images reflect a realistic
view of reality or a subjectively distorted one is to increase
your familiarity with your own imagery. Furthermore,
checking it for validity will increasingly enable you to distinguish when you are seeing clearly and when your perception is distorted by fears or desires.

The following exercise is particularly useful in evoking a
flow of inner images, and can also be good practice in allowing yourself to observe the images without interpretation. By working with a partner you also have the
added advantage of being able to give each other feedback
and discuss your responses to the images that come to
mind.

> Sitting opposite your partner (in a group setting it is
> preferable to choose someone you do not know), take
> a few minutes to become centered and quiet. Close
> your eyes and be aware of your breathing, and notice
> any physical sensations that are present for you at this
> moment. Be aware of any feelings that are present for
> you, and notice the thoughts that are going through

your mind. Be aware of how it feels to be you at this moment, and what your energy field feels like. If you were to visualize an energy field surrounding your body, what would it be like? Give yourself a few minutes of silence to be fully aware of your experience right now.

Open your eyes now and give your partner your full attention. Without talking, simply look at your partner and notice how you feel being with this person. In a receptive mode, simply allow this person into your awareness. Close your eyes again and see if you can get a clear picture of your partner in your mind's eye with your eyes closed. If some details are not clear, open your eyes again and fill them in. Look at your partner long enough and carefully enough to get a clear picture of what he or she looks like with your eyes closed.

For the remainder of this exercise your eyes can be either open or closed. Do not try to make anything happen. Simply notice what images come to mind when you are given a suggestion. If nothing comes to mind, that is O.K. Do not try to interpret or judge your images as they appear, simply notice them and let them be.

If this person were an animal, what type of animal would it be? If this person were a plant, what type of plant would it be? If this person were a landscape, what would it be? If this person were a body of water, what would it be? How deep? How clear? What temperature? How much movement? If this person were a light, what color and intensity would it be? If this person were a geometrical symbol, what would it be? If this person were a type of music, what would it be? If this person were a tool, what would it be? If this person were a character in history, who would it be? Can you visualize your partner as a little child? As a very old person? How do you experience your part-

ner's energy field? What is the energy field like between you—the energy field in which you both participate? Take a few minutes of silence now simply to be
quiet and receptive to any images that may emerge
spontaneously as you continue to focus your attention
on your partner.

Take as much time as you want to share with your
partner the images which emerged for you. You can
share any feelings you have about the images, but *do
not* attempt to interpret them.

You may have found that during this exercise some images just popped into your mind without any effort on
your part, while others seemed more difficult, and you
began thinking about what image would be appropriate.
You may also have noticed that if an image appeared
spontaneously and you did not like it, you tried to reject it
and get something else. The first image may have been so
persistent that it would not go away, or you may have
managed to erase it and substitute something you liked
better. The first image is the best one to work with. If you
did not like it, you were probably interpreting it. For example, if you got the image of a cow for the woman sitting opposite you when you tried to think of an animal,
you may have rejected it, judging it to be uncomplimen-
tary, not wanting to hurt her feelings. That is a judgment
and interpretation of the image. Images have both positive
and negative aspects and may be interpreted differently in
different contexts. For example, a cow might very well
connote serenity, contentment, and life-sustaining qualities. Similarly, the image of a snake might be considered
negative or frightening, whereas it has a long history as a
symbol of wisdom and healing power.

Working with a series of images, like working with a
series of dreams, can give a fuller and more distinct picture of a particular person than a single metaphoric image.
When you read the following response to the exercise

above, notice what sort of person emerges for you out of the descriptive imagery.

> I see you as a lioness, a bay tree, a landscape of rolling foothills by the sea, a waterfall, clear and cold and turbulent, a laser beam, a blue color, a triangle, a Bach concerto, a wrench, a pioneer in the Old West. I see you as a quiet, shy, frightened child, and as an old woman with a twinkle in her eye. Your energy field seems strong and vibrant and permeable. I am strongly aware of your presence in my space.

Here is a different picture:

> I see you as a bear, a gnarled old cypress, a restless ocean, cold and murky, a desert landscape, flickering firelight, yellow-gold, an oval, acid rock music, a bull-dozer, a Roman soldier. I see you as an energetic, aggressive little boy, and a wrinkled, sad, wise old man. Your energy field feels solid, I seem to bounce off, and I don't feel connected.

Sometimes a composite picture emerges in which all the images have a very definitive tone. For example,

> I see you as a deer, a daisy, a mountain meadow, a quiet pond, warm and still, not clear, a soft lamp, a rosy glow, a sphere, a Chopin sonata, a garden trowel, an Indian princess. As a child I see you playing with other children in a make-believe play. As an old woman I see you surrounded by a big family. I experience your energy field as soft and warm, it seems to flow in waves around both of us. I feel comfortable with you.

It is particularly interesting to do this exercise in a workshop with someone who is a complete stranger to you. By evoking imagery you can learn a lot about how much you can perceive without talking, if you take the time to really pay attention to another person. Sometimes the images that appear have a definite relationship to a person's life, such as a woman who was seen as an orchid, and later told her partner that her hobby was growing orchids. Another person described a landscape with a stream and a bridge which had been a familiar landscape to his partner as a child. Frequently images that appear may have personal significance for the individual. One man who was perceived as a bull, for instance, said he had been raised on a cattle ranch and, being interested in astrology, identified himself as a Taurus.

On one occasion, when I was doing this exercise with a group and I sat down with someone I had never seen before, he told me that during the period of silence he had a clear image of a three-petaled lotus with a circle in it. As he described the image in detail, I was amazed at the accuracy with which he was describing the symbol I had visualized that morning as part of a yogic meditation practice. I have since learned that this kind of thing happens quite regularly, and it therefore seems less amazing but nonetheless intriguing.

The imagery itself may take many different forms. When asked to imagine a type of music, for example, you may hear a particular piece of music and be unable to identify it; another person may visualize a score. Another may think of a word, such as *jazz*, without any auditory or visual concomitant. There is no right way to get an image. What is useful about this exercise, apart from what you can learn about your ability to see more than you thought you could see, is that it can help you to become familiar with your particular style of imagining. The more familiar you are with your own process, the easier it will be for you to distinguish accurate, intuitive perceptions from projections and fantasies.

Sometimes two people working together in this exercise will get the same image. The question that often comes up then is: "Is that your image or mine?" Sometimes it can be ascribed to coincidence or personal resemblance, but whenever it happens take notice of your feelings. Do you feel possessive about a particular image? If I see you as a river and you see me as a river, is that your river or mine? If we see each other as pyramids and you have been reading about pyramids, does that make it your image? Are you seeing me as a pyramid just because you have pyramids on your mind (projection)? Am I picking up that image telepathically and reflecting it back? These are frequently asked questions that cannot be answered definitively. Nevertheless, two people giving each other feedback can help clear up any confusion. In fact, it is both unnecessary and counterproductive to establish ownership of images. The whole process works best when it is a matter of sharing and participation rather than giving and taking. Giving up the desire to be right usually allows the process to flow much more easily, and can be very rewarding. Consider the images as pictures that emerge when you and your partner are together. When you focus attention on your partner you can put aside concern with your self and let it lie dormant for a while. It is easier to be fully aware of someone if you take time at the outset to tune into your own feelings, thoughts, and sensations. Then you know where you are, and personal concerns are less likely to intrude as distractions.

Often participants in this exercise are surprised at how relevant the imagery turns out to be. Not only are scenes from childhood often depicted accurately, but the type of music, or the plant, for example, is often one which the person being observed particularly likes, or is strongly associated with. People can see each other much more clearly than they admit. Who you are is quite apparent to anyone who cares to take the time to quiet down and allow the experience of being with you to be the focus of their attention. Similarly, you can know much more about other people than you usually notice or articulate. You can sense what someone is like simply by being with them. You do not have to talk or ask questions. The quality of a person's presence can be clearly perceived by anyone who cares to tune in to their intuitive abilities.

You can check out your intuitive perceptions of another person with a very simple, yet powerful exercise in which you simply tell another person how you see him or her, and ask for feedback. It will be especially useful as a tool for learning about your own perceptions if you do not read beyond the instructions until after you have tried it. The fewer preconceptions you have about what you should say, or how you should see another person, the more spontaneous you will be and the more scope you will be giving to your own ability to verbalize intuitive perceptions, rather than using someone else's forms of expression. Working with groups I give the following instructions:

Choose a partner and sit opposite this person without talking. Close your eyes and take a few minutes to get centered. The following centering exercise is very effective: With eyes closed, focus your attention on a point in the center of your belly, two inches below the navel, and two inches in toward the spine. Breathe into that center, imagining that you are drawing energy into that center as you inhale, and allowing it to flow out from that center as you exhale. Feel the energy flowing throughout your body, drawing the energy in on the inhale, allowing it to flow out on the exhale. Pause. Move your attention now to a point in the center of your chest, to the heart center. Imagine there a flame which increases in warmth and brightness as you inhale, drawing energy into that center as you inhale, letting it radiate out as you exhale. Pause. Move your attention now to a point in the center of your forehead, between the eyebrows, and in toward the center of your head. Imagine there a light which increases in brightness and intensity as you inhale, drawing energy into that center on the inhale, letting it radiate out on the exhale. Holding all three centers in your awareness, take two or three breaths. Pause. Be aware of how it feels to be you at this moment.

Open your eyes now and look at your partner. Decide which one of you will talk first. If your partner is going to talk first, your job is to simply listen, without giving any feedback, while your partner talks for about two minutes. No feedback means no smiles, nods or "uh-huh's." Simply be present with your partner, and hear what he or she has to say. If you are the one who is talking, take two minutes to tell your partner how you see him or her. When the two minutes are up, close your eyes and be silent. Allow yourself to be quiet and get in touch with your deeper self. Give yourself two minutes of silence in which you wait for something to come to you from your deeper self that you would like to say to your partner. Tell your partner what you want to say and return to silence.

Now reverse roles, so that the person who spoke listens to how he or she is perceived by the other for two minutes. Take two minutes of silence to get in touch with the deeper self, share anything you want to say and be silent again. Take a few minutes now with your eyes closed to reflect on the process you have just been through. Think about what you have heard and what you have said, and reflect on how much of it you think was perception and how much was projection. When you have had a chance to review the experience in your own mind, open your eyes and share your responses with your partner. Now is the time to give each other as much feedback as possible.

When you have completed the process, check the accuracy of your perceptions and take special note of your own emotional responses to what your partner said about you. Did you feel you were perceived accurately? Is there a difference between the way you wish to be seen and the way you really are? Do you feel uncomfortable if someone says something complimentary about you? Are you willing to acknowledge what is true about yourself, or do you have a tendency to deny positive observations as well as negative ones? Sometimes it may seem easier to put yourself down than to acknowledge your assets. Were your observations of your partner primarily physical, emotional, mental, or spiritual? All perceptions are limited. How do you limit yours? Does it seem safer to stick to observations of a physical, concrete nature? Do you have to have a reason or an explanation for your observation? Did you share all the images or metaphors that came to mind during this exercise? Do you feel that what you see in the other person is also a part of yourself? Does this person make a good mirror for you?

Of course, you see your partner only through the windows of your own eyes, and your perceptions are necessarily colored by your own physical, mental, and emotional state. This is why doing the centering exercise first is useful, for it can clear away at least some of the internal distractions. Be honest with yourself and allow yourself to recognize your hits as well as your misses when you make an observation. In a structured exercise such as this you have made an agreement with your partner to try a riskier way to get to know him or her than the usual social games of etiquette. When you have finished the exercise, you will have spent only a few minutes with this person, yet you may feel that you know each other very well. All you have done is to make a space for an intuitive mode of knowing which, while it is there all the time, is often ignored when the silence and the space between you and another is filled with superficial chatter about other things and other times.

This exercise is clearly present-oriented. For a few minutes it allows you to focus exclusively on what is going on with you and your partner. You are not distracted by talking or listening to stories about the past or expectations of the future. The space in this moment is where you can become conscious of the intuitive knowing that lies beneath ordinary conversation and behind worldly concerns about past and future.

You may feel that such an exercise is not really valid because anything you might say could fit another person if you talk in generalities and avoid specifics. Nonetheless, the exercise will have as much validity for you as you are willing to give it. How much you learn from it about your own intuitive ways of knowing will depend on how much you are willing to risk in the process. Again, do not interpret too quickly what you observe. Rather than merely telling another person that he or she is this or that, be conscious of the fact that you are only offering your particular point of view, and preface your statements with, "I see you as . . ." rather than saying, "You are . . ." Most of us are eager to know how others see us, although we may feel apprehensive when facing the prospect of straight, honest feedback. "Will my partner see all my shortcomings?" "Will my partner see how scared I am?"

In addition, this exercise is useful in developing your capacity for self-observation in the listening role. What feelings came up when your partner was talking about you? Were you pleased, frightened, angry, embarrassed, or all of these?

To illustrate this aspect of the exercise, check your reactions to the description that follows by imagining that you are the person about whom the following observations are made:

> I see you as strong but uncertain, not sure of what is expected. I feel that you are cautious, but curious and willing to take some risks. You are caring and sensitive, afraid of violence and anger. You have been disappointed and sometimes depressed. Right now you may be hesitating or experiencing some inner conflict about making a decision that could change your life. You know what you have to do, but you keep trying to figure out if it is the "right" thing, wanting some reassurance. You are like a young tree, bending in the wind, putting down deep roots and growing stronger. Silence: From my deeper self I want to say that I like you, I feel good with you.

Reading this example of what one person might say to another in this exercise may not seem very significant. Indeed, the things said here could fit many people. There is no specific perception such as, "I see you driving a small red sports car," which could turn out to be true or false. If specific images do appear, it is a good idea to check them out with your partner in order to learn about the reliability of such flashes. Many times they are correct, and it is only through trial and error, many trials and many errors, that you can begin to make a subjective distinction between projections and perceptions. However, the point of this exercise is not to attempt to guess facts about your partner, but to express your perceptions and responses as directly as possible, for your mutual benefit in learning about how intuition works.

In considering such generalities as the ones above, be sure to note not only the content, but the feeling conveyed, and the fact that whatever emerges does so in a particular context between two particular individuals at one particular time. Given the instructions, "Tell your partner how you see him or her," a person can say almost anything. If you are doing the talking, remember that what you choose to say also says something about you and the way you see others—in this case, your partner. One always reveals something about oneself in talking. Indeed, this exercise can help one see how much is revealed by one's presence alone, even when nothing is said. You don't have to know how to read body language to be able to get an impression of what another person is like. Learning to articulate and communicate your impressions may be more difficult. If you tend to notice physical attributes, movements, and posture, you may comment on them. If you tend to be empathetic and can sense how other people feel, or what moods and attitudes they have, you may comment on these. If you tend to pick up on people's thoughts and ideas, try to express what you think they are. In all cases, if you avoid structuring the form of the observation and simply allow yourself to report whatever appears, you have a good opportunity to see how your intuition works. Given all the things you could observe about another human being, what do you choose to comment on in the first two minutes? What presents itself to you in this particular Gestalt?

The difficulty with this exercise is not so much the inability to observe, but rather the lack of practice in articulating what you observe. First impressions may change with further acquaintance, but frequently they last and are confirmed when you get to know another person better. Unless you are willing to trust some of these impressions when they occur, it will be difficult for you to distinguish the reliable observations from the projections and distortions. The willingness to be wrong, to make mistakes and give up the attachment to being right, is one factor that accelerates learning. The more you are willing to risk stating intuitive impressions, the more you will be able to trust them and know when they are accurate and when they are questionable.

Symbolic Images of Intuition

There is a distinct difference between images that convey intuitive insights into one's own psyche or another individual's state of being, and images which symbolize intuition itself. Remember that intuition as a way of knowing transcends intellect and reason. It goes beyond what is comprehensible to the rational mind. Sometimes it appears to be in conflict with reason, but more often it is simply outside the ways of knowing that depend on ordinary sensory channels for information. Intuition is sometimes symbolized as an eagle, a farsighted bird which can see a very long distance from a very great height. More often, intuition is symbolized by the third eye, or the eye of inner vision. This eye of inner vision can be trained through meditation to see into your own mind and the nature of reality, and is said to be omniscient. It symbolizes insight, the single vision of the mystic which penetrates behind the veil of apparent differences and dualities, to see the unity in all existence.

Images of intuition such as the circle, the cross, and the triangle are frequently found in religious symbols. A familiar one is the eye in the triangle portrayed on the dollar bill. According to Jung,[9] a symbol is a vehicle for conveying concepts which cannot be fully defined or comprehended. The symbol always points beyond itself, to a deeper meaning which eludes intellectual understanding. Thus symbols form a bridge between what is known and what is unknown, giving form to the formless and expanding the horizon of inner vision.

The purpose of discussing symbolic images of intuition here is not to give an exhaustive review of mythological or religious images which pertain to intuitive modes of knowing. Rather it is to suggest a way for you to discover the symbols that can help develop your intuition and expand your awareness of what you already know.

If visualization is easy for you, you may be able to come up with a variety of symbolic images, simply by focusing on what intuition means to you and waiting for a visual image or a metaphor to appear. If this seems difficult to you, the following exercise may facilitate the process.

Close your eyes and imagine that you are descending a long staircase, very slowly, one step at a time. You may want to count the steps as you walk down. At the bottom of the stairs there is a door. The door is closed. Over the door is written the word INTUITION. Someone will bring you the key to the door. When you have the key, unlock the door, open it, and go through it. See what you find on the other side. Explore the space in which you find yourself, getting to know it. Look around to see if there is anything there that you would like to bring back with you. Take your time. There is no hurry. Pause. Get ready to come back now. Come back through the door, close it and go back up the stairs. Remember that you can return to this place whenever you choose.

Responses to this fantasy vary widely. For people who are comfortable with their intuition, it can simply be an amplification or celebration of the awareness they already have. Sometimes they report feelings of joy and bliss in association with intergalactic travel, flashes of brilliant light, pleasurable rushes of energy, intense color, fireworks, and occasionally a direct experience of a formless void. In such experiences the instructions to bring something back may feel inappropriate and simply be ignored. Sometimes a symbolic representation of sun, moon, or stars may be brought back as a reminder of the experience.

More often, this fantasy will elicit imagery that carries the mind out of the confines of ordinary time and space, and yet is represented by more concrete images such as a view of the earth as a planet, far-reaching visions over great distances, crystal balls, magic mirrors, or reflective surfaces of water or other devices that are used for extending the powers of inner vision in myths and fairy tales. This type of image, even when consciously forgotten, may reappear spontaneously when a person is invited to explore more fully his or her unconscious imagery associated with intuition. Objects imbued with magical power are frequently brought back as the unfamiliarity of intuition is commonly associated with magic and the occult.

An essential part of expanding your ability to use intuition lies in its demystification. Understanding how psychic energy can be invested and stored in physical objects can allow you to work with symbolic objects without falling into superstitious fears or simply discounting such images as meaningless and insignificant. Symbolic images become devices for extending the mind beyond the boundaries of logical thought. The symbol invested with psychic energy has transformative power and leads beyond itself into the mystery of the unknown. In this way it serves the function of making intuition more accessible to consciousness.

Occasionally the fantasy may evoke imagery which can be frightening, such as darkness, falling, dissolving, black holes, dungeons, monsters, etc. Even these images are useful, however, for anyone willing to work through the fears they represent. Remember that whatever appears is your own thought form, and the fear that produced it was there before you imagined the specific form. When you have a specific image to work with, you can begin the process of taking responsibility and overcoming it. Such fears cannot be dismissed or bypassed, and thus such images can give one an indication of precisely what work needs to be done in order to overcome them. Any transpersonal experience involving the extension of consciousness beyond the usual ego boundaries can be either ecstatic or terrifying. Fears and anxiety are obstacles to releasing potential, and everyone experiences them in one form or another. When confronted with a fearful image one can either pull back or take the opportunity to work through it. The choice of when and how to deal with it is a personal one, yet the imagery can always be useful in deepening one's experience and understanding of oneself.

In other words, self-awareness is the ground from which intuition comes to full fruition. Honoring and valuing the nonrational aspects of oneself inevitably calls for confronting all kinds of fears—fear of letting go, fear of dying, fear of loneliness, fear of disorientation, fear of unknowns, fear of evil, fear of punishment, fear of power, etc.

Some basic rules for dealing with fearful imagery when it appears in a fantasy are as follows:

1. Open your eyes and discontinue the fantasy. This should be done only when you choose not to employ one of the other methods suggested for working with it within the fantasy.

2. Find a competent guide whom you trust and who can go with you if you want to continue this exploration.

3. If you do not feel overwhelmed by the imagery, examine it and describe it in detail.

4. If there is one figure which is threatening, real or unreal, engage the figure in dialogue and ask what it wants.

5. If it is some sort of creature, look in its eyes. Find out what it likes to eat. Feed it.

6. If you imagine you are in a dark place, visualize yourself leading or taking the threatening creature into the sunlight. See if it changes in any way. Talk to it.

7. Become the threatening figure in your imagination. How does this creature feel?

8. If you do not think you can manage by yourself, bring someone into your fantasy to help you or to be with you.

9. Remember that in fantasy anything is possible. You can avail yourself of a magic wand or some other power you may wish to imagine.

10. Call on supernatural power for help, whatever guide or teacher is yours (e.g., Christ, Buddha, or God).

11. Imagine the whole scene or the threatening figure suffused in white light.

12. Do not kill. In the inner world, nothing dies. It can be transformed, but killing does not necessarily effect a transformation and the fear will return in another form. Remember, everything is a part of you.

One might assume that one has control over fantasies, but the control may be superficial and ineffectual if one is not willing to go deeper into the inner world, which inevitably leads to unknown aspects of oneself. Fear of self-knowledge is hardly new or unusual.

Abraham Maslow called attention to the fact that we fear our highest possibilities as well as our lowest ones. Maslow called this defense against accepting responsibility for developing unused potentialities an "evasion of des-

tiny," or "running away from one's own best talents."[10] In
fantasies one can easily recognize that fear may be aroused
not only by a sense of impending disaster, but also by feelings of wonder and awe. Generally speaking, when images
are positive (i.e., beautiful, nurturing, or inspiring), they
do not pose a problem. However, it is best to be aware
that identification with positive images can be a trap. For
instance, if one becomes attached to an unrealistic self-
image, sooner or later it will have to be dropped. As in the
process of learning to disidentify from emotions, working
with images for awakening intuition includes both
identification with them and disidentification from them
as contents of consciousness.

If you think you need help to overcome resistances,
don't be embarrassed to ask for it. We all need help in
one way or another from time to time. The arrogance
implied in trying to do it alone is only another obstacle to
be overcome. Trust your intuition to let you know when
it is appropriate to seek help and when you need to work
alone. Both are integral to growth and self-realization.

5

Dreams and Intuition

The center that I cannot find
is known to my unconscious mind.

—W. H. AUDEN: *The Labyrinth*

Since ancient times, dreams have been honored as a source of wisdom and guidance in life. Messages from the gods, later translated as messages from the unconscious, have come through dreams in all cultures. "For all of us living the ordinary world," says Ann Faraday, "the dreaming mind is capable of adding a whole dimension of wisdom to life which is equivalent to the discovery of an inner guru within each one of us."[1] Although claims that voices of the gods can be reduced to right-hemisphere activity[2] or that sleep is the special province of the right brain[3] are oversimplifications, the fact remains that dreams are imagistic formulations of what one knows intuitively. Dreams are a readily accessible language of intuition, and expanding awareness of dreams expands intuition as well.

Freud called dreams the royal road to the unconscious, and although he denied any supernatural manifestations, he saw dreams following the laws of the human spirit that

he described as "akin to the divine."[4] Psychoanalytic
dream theorists have been predominantly concerned with
the psychological meaning of dream content. Freud
thought that dreams could be interpreted as disguised
wish fulfillment, and favored free association as a method
of interpretation. He describes the necessary conditions for
this method as follows: "We must aim at bringing about
two changes in him [the patient]: an increase in the attention he pays to his own psychical perceptions and the
elimination of the criticism by which he normally sifts the
thoughts that occur to him . . . It is necessary to insist
explicitly on his renouncing all criticism of the thoughts
that he perceives."[5] Freud also encouraged self-observation
in working with dreams: "I . . . am prepared to find that
the same piece of content may conceal a different meaning when it occurs in various people or in various contexts.
. . . In my judgment the situation is in fact more favora-
ble in the case of self-observation than in that of other
people."[6]

Jung's approach to dreams differs from Freud's. He
believed dream content did not necessarily conceal or dis-
guise psychological truth, but actually revealed it. A dream
might express a hidden conflict or problem, or it might
point the way to some unrecognized possibility of future
development. Jung felt dreams should be interpreted in
whatever way the dreamer found most useful, and insisted
that there was no such thing as a correct interpretation.
He wrote: "No dream symbol can be separated from the
individual who dreams it, and there is no definite or
straightforward interpretation of any dream."[7]

Max Zeller, a Jungian analyst, writes that man has
difficulty relating to dreams because he no longer under-
stands the language of images. "Images happen to us,"
says Dr. Zeller. "They make up the tapestry of our inner
life, surround us as our inner world, and silently talk to us
in their picture language, the language of the unknown
background. They express another reality, another dimension that cannot be approached according to the laws that

are valid in the outside world. . . . The unconscious calls us with its images, and thereby reveals the forces at work in the psyche."[8] Through dreams the unconscious also reveals unsuspected resources of inner wisdom.

Dreams also reflect the dreamer's attitudes and current concerns. Jung maintained that dreams restore psychic balance by compensating for deficiencies in the personality, and may also warn of dangers inherent in current situations.[9] Gestalt dream interpretation, as developed by Frederick Perls, is likewise present-oriented and focuses on what the dream reveals about the dreamer and his or her problems. In Gestalt dream work, the dreamer is instructed to identify with every image in the dream, assuming that everything in the dream represents a disowned or projected aspect of the self. In this way the dream provides a means of expanding self-knowledge and changing self-image.

Dreams are, moreover, the most common altered state of consciousness in which ESP phenomena appear.[10] Research at Maimonides Dream Laboratory in New York[11] investigated the occurrence of telepathy in dreams, but precognition is apparently the most frequent type of ESP in dreams.[12] Precognitive dreams are dreams of future events, or dreams that come true in waking life. Psychic dreams are those which transcend time and space by providing accurate information about what is happening at other times in other places. Dream consciousness, typically intuitive, is not bound by time and space. Many *déjà vu* experiences can be accounted for by remembering dreams. People who record their dreams and have clear recall of dream landscapes sometimes dream of places and events which come into their lives at a later time.

In yoga psychology dreams are understood as a combination of images from the personal unconscious depicting current problems and situations, and an opportunity for contact with the transpersonal field of consciousness, which has not been integrated into awareness. Dreams are thus said to communicate intuitions as well as representing personal problems.[13] Some yogis can maintain alert, waking consciousness in the sleep state as indicated by the appearance of delta brain-wave rhythms monitored by biofeedback researchers.[14] This ability to enter a physical state of sleep while remaining fully conscious enables the yogi to consciously experience the dream state and to control the character of dreams simply by willing it.

In *Creative Dreaming* Patricia Garfield gives complete instructions for increasing your capacity for lucid dreaming (i.e., maintaining awareness that you are dreaming while you are dreaming).[15] This is a way of expanding consciousness in the dream state that is possible for anyone. Tibetan dream yoga also suggests a useful reversal in working with dreams: Consider your dream world as the true reality, and your ordinary waking life as a dream. Are you willing to take responsibility for the reality you create in your dreams? *The Tibetan Book of the Dead* gives these instructions: "O nobly-born, whatever fearful and terrifying visions thou mayst see, recognize them to be thine own thought-forms."[16]

Do you enjoy your dreams? Are you aware that you are dreaming when you dream? Would you like to change, repeat, or continue a particular dream? Would you like to use your dreams as an inexhaustible wellspring of creativity? All these things are possible, and giving your dreams the attention they deserve is the first step.

Laboratory research has demonstrated that everyone dreams every night, but many people do not recall their dreams. If you are one of those people who has difficulty remembering dreams, there are several methods which can help you remember them. The easiest method is simply to lie quietly in bed upon waking and review the dream fragments which are still accessible before you start your routine of waking activity. Even dream fragments can be used as doorways into the unconscious. Any dream can serve as a starting point for an exploration of the psyche, and can help you understand the workings of your own mind. Sometimes you may find yourself having spontaneous associations to dream images which seem to amplify the meaning of the dream, but associations may also lead you away from the dream, so be aware that the first task is to remember the dream just as it occurred.

A useful practice is to keep a paper and pencil or a tape recorder next to your bed in order to record your dreams immediately upon waking. You might wake up in the middle of the night, remember a dream vividly, then go back to sleep. By morning you might well have forgotten the dream, in spite of having been sure that you would remember it. The same thing happens with dreams that you remember in the morning. If you do not record them right away, they tend to fade. You might want to try an experiment with yourself: Write down a dream immediately upon waking, and then write it down again later in the day, from memory, without referring to your first account. It can be surprising to see how much memory changes experience.

A more drastic method of improving dream recall is to set an alarm at various intervals during the night. Your chances of being awakened in the middle of a dream that you will remember are good. You might prefer to have a friend awaken you when rapid eye movements during sleep indicate that you are dreaming. Some people find they can more easily remember dreams during naps in the daytime. Even if you are not in the habit of napping, you might want to try it for the purpose of remembering your dreams more clearly.

Another method for improving dream recall is to give yourself the suggestion before you go to sleep that you will remember your dreams. You can give yourself the suggestion often during the day as well, but repeating it just as you are dropping off to sleep, when your body is relaxed, is particularly effective. In fact, dream recall is often improved simply by wanting to improve it. Ann Faraday reminds us that the basic factor that determines whether a person remembers dreams or not is the same as that which determines other memory, namely degree of interest. Dr.

Faraday says nonrecallers are sometimes surprised to learn that failure to recall dreams is simply due to lack of interest, yet many report remembering dreams immediately after discussing the subject.[17] One of my students in a college class, a woman in her fifties who said she had never remembered a dream in her life, started remembering them as a result of a classroom discussion on dreams in which she learned that it was possible to do so. At the end of the semester she told me that she was thoroughly enjoying her dreams, and felt that her ability to remember them greatly enriched her life, and also made her intuition more accessible.

Other activities that contribute to dream awareness and recall are reading books about dreams, talking to friends or family about dreams, and simply valuing your dreams. Dreams are metaphors of life situations, and as such you can consider them stories you are telling yourself. Because dreams seldom make logical sense, any form of dream work involves intuitive faculties. It is best to avoid literal or cookbook interpretations of symbols appearing in dreams, since each image derives its meaning from the context of your life. Dreams are always true in the sense that they always pertain to your life when they occur, and paying attention to them nurtures psychological growth and integration.[18] Dreams are less likely to be products of personal wishes than fantasies, and it is useful to remember that a dream can have several levels of meaning simultaneously. Writing about the personal uses of dreams, psychologist Wilson Van Dusen says: "The main value of the dream can be obtained when the individual can read back the meanings of his own dream. . . . The only meanings in a dream that you can use are those that you can relate to your own life."[19] "In general," says Dr. Van Dusen, "the dream reflects your deepest thought. Its wisdom may well transcend your ordinary understanding."[20]

As you become more conscious *of* your dreams, you may also become more conscious *in* your dreams. Thus you may have an increasing number of lucid dreams, in which you know you are dreaming. When you have a lucid dream you can change it and shape it in any way you wish. Learning to control your dreams takes time and requires patience, but the rewards make it worthwhile. For example, you can decide to confront a threatening figure in a dream instead of running away, and see what happens. The effects of working consciously in your dreams are not limited to changing your dream reality. When you change your dreams, your waking consciousness also changes. Conversely, if you make changes in your waking life and consciousness, your dreams will change because dreams and waking life reflect each other.

Increased receptivity to dreams in waking life contributes to increased effectiveness in dream activity, increased lucidity, and dream control. Instead of experiencing dreams as happening to you, you can begin to recognize that you are actually the producer, director, actor, *and* audience in every show. Do you still experience yourself as a victim in your dreams? In waking life? Would you like to rewrite the script? You can make any changes you like. You already have all the information you need. Your dreams provide you with the working material, and you can begin immediately.

Anyone who has kept a dream journal, recording dreams on a daily basis, or worked with dreams over a period of time, will know intuitively when a dream is particularly significant. Some dreams are charged with immediately recognizable emotional intensity, even if the meaning of the dream is not fully understood. Recurring dreams often have this quality, and the fact that they recur may be attributed to the inability of the conscious mind to comprehend what the unconscious is attempting to convey, or to a resistance against the existential message of the dream. Recurring dreams may also represent recurring patterns of response in which one can feel stuck. When the message is understood, the dream changes. For example, a woman who had recurring dreams of fires which she was continually struggling to put out, eventually realized that the fires symbolized her creative impulses which she had tried to stifle. When she acknowledged the futility of her attempts to live her life strictly in accordance with preconceived ideals regardless of her feelings and desires, she began to make some changes in her life and the dream changed. Gradually, as she found ways to express her inner self, the fires became less threatening; eventually the dream disappeared altogether.

In working with your own dreams, either alone or with others, remember that oversimplified interpretations may rob you of the more subtle implications of a particular dream. When using dreams for the purpose of expanding intuition and self-knowledge, hold rational, critical judgments in abeyance while exploring the emotional and intuitive levels of the dream.

Gestalt methods for dream work are particularly effective for working on the emotional level. Gestalt dream work involves identifying with every person and/or object in a dream and describing oneself as the other in terms of affect, function, relationship, and as an observer of the dream action. If, for example, your dream takes place in a house, you would close your eyes and describe yourself as the house, in the first person, present tense. One might say, for instance, "I am an old, run-down house, badly in need of repairs." After describing physical details, you can proceed to expressing your feelings about yourself as the house, and your feelings about the content of the dream, always from the point of view of the house. The perspective thus shifts from one in which the ego, usually identified as the dreamer, is regarding all other dream images as separate from itself, to one in which ego boundaries dissolve and you as the dreamer are identified with every image in the dream, no matter how minute, insignificant, distasteful, or grandiose.

When dream images appear as threatening or fearful, as they inevitably do from time to time, the process of identifying with the threatening figure can give the dreamer a new awareness of repressed aspects of the personality which he or she may be reluctant to own. Dreams of being pursued by a person or a monster are very common, and may be obvious examples of personified inner conflict. For instance, young women often report dreams of being chased by a threatening male figure. If a woman who has such a dream is willing to see the figure as a representation of her own masculine energy which she is afraid to own, she may be able to incorporate it and become more assertive and less frightened in her waking life. If she can *imagine* how it feels to be strong and powerful, she is on the way to creating those feelings in herself.

This is not the only way to work with or interpret this type of dream. All of your dreams must be considered in the context of your whole life. In other words, the initial step of identification may simply reveal to you that you are the victimizer as well as the victim, the cop as well as the robber, the creator as well as the destroyer in every dream experience. By owning those aspects of the self which one denies even to oneself and projects onto others whom one dislikes, one can begin the process of personal integration. This is also a way to become more familiar with how it feels to know something by identifying with it rather than describing or talking about it, thus activating the intuitive mode.

Your willingness to take responsibility for everything in your dream, considering every image as your reflection and creation, allows you to become more aware of the ways in which you shape your reality in both dream and waking consciousness. As you become more conscious in your dreams you can do anything you want. You can change your dreams if you really intend to do so. You need not feel victimized by your dreams if you are willing to acknowledge your capacity to exercise your own volition. Becoming conscious in your dreams does not imply that you will dream only pleasant dreams. Nor does it imply that you should control your dreams. You may learn more from your dreams when you do not attempt to control them. The issue is one of taking responsibility for your dreams, accepting the fact that whatever you may have dreamed, it is *your* dream. You may consider it a story you are telling yourself or a message your intuitive self is attempting to communicate to your rational consciousness. The more you are willing to consciously incorporate your dreams as an intrinsic part of yourself, the more your self-concept can expand to include what you may already intuit to be true—that your inner world reflects the universe. Everything is included.

Practice in identifying with various dream images is excellent practice for developing a subjective sense of the difference between direct intuitive knowing, which transcends subject/object separateness, and rational understanding. Intuitively, you know better than anyone else what meaning lies hidden within the sometimes bizarre contents of a dream, and identifying with the images brings this knowledge into conscious awareness. Thus by owning projections one also expands intuition.

Dream work sometimes includes continuing a dream in fantasy. An unresolved situation can thus be resolved or completed in imagination. You can, for instance, ask dream images to talk to each other, or to talk with you, the dreamer, in order to reveal themselves more completely. You will find that dream images readily respond to inquiries when they are treated as real rather than as "only" imaginary, and can thus expand more fully, instead of being limited by premature interpretation.

I have found this method useful both in individual dream work and in groups. When a person is working on a dream in a group, I suggest that other members of the group listen to the dream *as if* it were one of their own. In this way, everyone can participate through identification with the dreamer, relating the dream to their own experience rather than attempting to analyze it. For instance, the meaning of a brief dream recounted by a young woman in a dream group expanded considerably when she tried this method of continuation and identification. The dream was fleeting but vivid:

> I am in a very dark cave and I feel there are cobwebs around me. I am terrified of encountering a huge spider like one I read about in a story. I find myself increasingly entangled and sense the monster nearby. I feel trapped and helpless.

> When I tell the dream I can feel anxiety growing inside me. The image of the spider is vague, but as I imagine it, it gets clearer. I see a huge black spider with beady eyes and metallic legs. She is bigger than I am and will trap me. She catches me and wraps me up in cobwebs, so that I am tightly bound up in a sort of cocoon, and I cannot move. I feel paralyzed. I feel I cannot possibly identify with this hideous creature. I am stuck. I make a tremendous effort and begin to describe myself as the spider. My body is cumbersome, but I am shrewd and cunning. I wait in my cave for someone to wander in. I am pleased and excited whenever someone does come in and I can trap them. I do not want to eat my victims. I just wrap them up so they are paralyzed and can't get away. I am delighted to see this woman coming into my cave. I'll catch her and keep her here with me, safely wrapped up. The problem is that after my victims have been in captivity for a time they are no longer lively or interesting, and they eventually die, so I always need new victims. Anybody who comes in from out there brings light and life from outside, and that is what I crave, what I feed on.

At this point the dreamer was asked to continue the dream as a fantasy and was given the following suggestion: "How would it feel if you, as the spider, came out of the cave into the sunlight?"

> I feel very frightened. I am always dissatisfied in here but at least I am safe. I know my way around and sooner or later someone will wander in. I manage to stay alive. I am sure that if I go out of my cave I will be destroyed. I am so ugly, I cannot bear the thought of daylight. Someone will kill me. I will be crushed. I want to stay hidden. I would rather rot here in the dark than risk being dismembered out there. Slowly, very slowly, I begin to creep cautiously to the mouth

of the cave. Each step requires tremendous effort. I want to
run back and hide. When I look out the light is blinding,
and I scuttle back in, but not too far. Eventually, summon-
ing all my courage, I come out, and as I feel the warmth of
the sunlight, the heavy back armor of my body falls away and
a tiny, white, harmless spider emerges from the inside. As
the little white spider I am overjoyed to be free and to feel
the sunlight. I want to play, but I'm still afraid of being
crushed, feeling small and vulnerable. But I feel so good out
here . . . it is worth taking a chance!

Reflecting on this identification with the threatening
image and the continuation of the dream in imagination,
the dreamer made the following observations:

I feel that I have been through a tremendous emotional up-
heaval. The release I felt on coming out of the cave and
shedding the armor was expressed in a lot of tears. I see the
black spider as a symbol of all the negative, destructive aspects of the feminine. She is the possessive, destructive, cas-
trating mother. She is everything I hate in other women and
deny in myself. Yet I see now that she is fearsome only because she herself is so afraid. She tries to get what she wants
from life from other people, her victims, because she is
afraid of going out to get it for herself. When she does
come out of hiding she feels vulnerable, but she no longer
appears as threatening. The spider could be a symbol of
repressions which are destructive and paralyzing until I can
bring them to consciousness. Once I recognize them and
deal with them, they are stripped of their power and I have
more energy. The dreadful fear I felt in the cave is gone. If
I have the courage to be vulnerable, there is hope for new
life and relationship.

In this case the dreamer's willingness to identify with
the threatening image and to continue the dream in her
imagination not only gave her new insights into some of
her own negative attitudes and fears, but also provided her
with a liberating experience. Everyone experiences inner
struggles in attempts to overcome fear, both in the inner
world and in the outer world. It would have been easy for
the dreamer to have dismissed the image of the dream as

something which she had conjured up simply because she had read about such a creature, and thus have disregarded its symbolic significance in her life. The process of identification, however, generated the emotional response leading to a new realization of the implications of the dream for her own life.

Another symbolic dream involving an overwhelming sense of fear which was eventually transcended and successfully integrated was told as follows:

> I am struggling with a huge snake or serpent. I am on the side of a mountain and I grab the creature behind the head and fling it into the abyss. I gain some respite and try to get away, but I know it is hopeless. I am in a house and I see the creature outside. The doors and windows are locked, but that is no deterrent to the snake that comes in through the window. Panicked, I wake up.

When asked to identify with the snake in imagination, the dreamer said:

> I am very strong and powerful—also wise and cunning. I don't want to destroy you; I want you to accept me. When you reject me, you can't control me and I am dangerous. You can't get rid of me, you need me. I'll find you wherever you are, and thwart you unless you make friends with me. I can break down any barriers and haunt you as long as you don't realize that I *am* you. I am a powerful, driving force. I am sexual and sensual. When you run away from me you are running away from your own energy. I am destructive only when you do not use my strength.

In reflecting on this experience the dreamer remarked:

> I see that I must come to terms with my own inner drives and urges. I know the snake is a phallic symbol and also has some connection with healing in ancient Greece. I also know it is associated with rebirth, because of its ability to shed its skin.

Some weeks after doing this symbolic identification the dreamer again dreamed of a snake but it was no longer threatening.

Dream work is not always as dramatically symbolic as in the dreams described above. However, it can always give the dreamer some new insight about his or her current attitudes and the way they shape the circumstances in life which seem to be beyond conscious control.

For example, a woman in her late twenties who lived alone and consciously wanted very much to be married, was unable to maintain any lasting relationships with men. One night she dreamed that she had married Phil, a former boyfriend, but that immediately after the wedding he changed into a psychopath. She felt trapped and terrified. Working with this dream led her to recognize how frightened she was of intimacy, how she really saw marriage as a trap, and how she was afraid of her own anger and irrational impulses. After this she was willing to accept her living situation as what she really wanted. Becoming more conscious of her deep-seated fear of commitment to a long-term relationship enabled her to confront it, and it gradually diminished.

If you have difficulty remembering dreams, personification of a dream fragment may help you recognize whatever resistance you may have to working with dream material. One man who only dimly remembered a fragment of a dream which he felt was useless, became the dream itself. Asking himself, as the dream, why he was so elusive, he replied that he would not reveal himself until the dreamer was ready to hear what it had to say. The dialogue was enough to trigger the recognition that he was in fact attempting to confront aspects of himself which he had not been prepared to deal with earlier.

The Gestalt method of working with a dream by identifying with the various images is especially useful in working on personal integration. However, there may be more to a dream than the portrayal of projected parts of the personality. Some dreams clearly pertain to the reality of everyday life, and include strong feelings of aggression and anxiety which are apt to be repressed in waking consciousness. Some dream images may also transcend egocentric self-concepts, and expand awareness of transpersonal potentials. Appropriate methods of dream work should be chosen for different types of dreams. For example, when the reality of everyday life is portrayed in a dream, you can simply notice what the dream says about it, without attempting to interpret it symbolically.

Whatever level of dream work you feel is appropriate for a particular dream, leave your conclusions about the dream open-ended. Your intuition may well expand the meaning of the dream after you have finished "working" with it. In *The Interpretation of Dreams*, Freud says: "It is in fact never possible to be sure that a dream has been completely interpreted."[21] One does not have to agree with his views on dream interpretation to recognize the validity of this observation. Even when the meaning seems obvious, remember that the obvious interpretation may conceal a deeper meaning.

One way of avoiding premature or limited interpretations, thus allowing your intuition to expand the meaning of a dream without verbal interference, is to draw the images of a dream. The drawing does not have to be an artistic production. Actually, the less concerned you are with how it looks, the more freely you can express the feeling or tone of the dream in the drawing. Natalie Rogers, a feminist therapist in Sausalito, California, wrote about her own experience with this technique at a time in her life when she was attempting to integrate what she calls her intuitive, receptive, sensual, spiritual side with her logical, pragmatic, linear, thinking side. She writes:

> One of the most important dreams of my life seems to symbolize just this point. The image I had, while asleep, was so startling I sat straight up in bed before I realized I was awake. The next morning I drew a picture of the dream image. It was difficult to describe the intensity with which I felt it.
>
> Two black cobras with tails coiled to support their upright bodies face each other, staring directly into each other's eyes. Their triangular heads jut forward from

highly arched necks, frozen in this encounter. Instead of
the cobra hood these snakes have large oval breastplates
dramatically striped with yellow and black. A magnetic
push/pull pulsation vibrates between the serpents as
they are poised in this striking stance. They are framed,
in the background, by an immense, golden full moon.

That apparition has never left me. Drawing the image has
helped me remember it. The intense, positive energy between the two snakes had a powerful impact on me. These
two creatures were of almost equal strength and size. The
snake on the left is proud and strong, with neck and head
reaching forward. She has five yellow stripes, is slightly
smaller, and her head is less assertive. Her neck is not as
firmly attached to her body as is her twin's. In drawing this
picture I was totally unconscious of their differences until
months later. Now I wonder if the dream is partly a statement about the new-found strength of my psychic, feminine
side. The full moon in the background is an integrating circle encompassing the bodies of both.

After dreaming this, I became more aware of the snake
symbols in museums and books. They abound, of course. In
Man and His Symbols,[22] I had read of the serpent as existing in the myths of every culture as the symbol of the source
of energy, of cosmic forces. The snake assumes many forms,
including the two serpents intertwined around a wand which
becomes the caduceus (used as our medical symbol), the
symbol of healing, of fluidity, and of opposing forces balancing one another.

The snake, I understand, is also a symbol of transcendence
—a mediation between earth and heaven. Much of what
seems to be happening to me in my middle age is to become
more aware of that which is not earthbound.

My sense of my cobra dream was that of the opposing
forces within me framed by the larger feminine symbol, the
full moon. When these forces within confront each other
they create a dynamic vital energy.

Working with dreams by drawing, painting, or shaping
images in clay is particularly appropriate if you are working alone. You may, at times, choose to work alone, even
when you could easily tell your dream to a friend or a

member of your family, to give your own intuitive process the opportunity to unfold without external interference. If, however, you prefer to work on dreams with another person or in a dream group (i.e., a group formed for the specific purpose of working on dreams), the following guidelines can facilitate the process.

Whatever method of dream work is used, take a few minutes to quiet the mind and relax before recounting a dream. In a group setting, I ask participants to close their eyes for a brief period of quiet relaxation and give the following instructions:

> Remember how you felt last night when you were ready to go to sleep. Remember the last thing you were aware of before you fell asleep. How does your body feel when you are just drifting off to sleep? Allow yourself to enjoy the feeling of relaxation as you remember the feeling of falling asleep, and rest for a few moments. When you are ready to recount your dream, tell it in the first person, present tense, as if it were happening now. If you are listening to someone telling a dream, close your eyes and listen to it imaginatively, as if it were your dream. If you are telling a dream, begin when you feel ready.

When you read the dream below try following these instructions and imagining that it is your dream. Any dream image can be related subjectively to your life. What significance could it have for you?

"I am in a city, on a college campus, looking for a building. I am with a group of friends. (I don't know who they are.) I ask directions from someone passing by. I am told we must drive out a certain boulevard. We all get into a car and as we drive the road changes from a city street to a bumpy, unpaved country road. In the distance I see a building. I get out of the car and go in. My friends wait in the car. The building looks like a medical building and is very quiet. It seems no one is here. Then I see someone

wearing a white coat. I ask about the building I am looking for and he says it is right next door. I had not noticed
it when I drove up, but there it is. I go out of this building and into the other one. Yes, this is the building I was
looking for. It is brand-new. It is pleasant and modern and
has thick carpet on the floor. I am pleased as I walk
around inside discovering different rooms. It is ready for
occupancy, but is not yet in use."

It was easy for this dreamer to relate the dream images
to recent events in her life. She was ready for a change,
but had not yet decided what she wanted to do next. As
she worked on the dream she realized that she had known
that she wanted to start a new project at work which
would eventually involve a number of people working together in an educational service. As in the dream, she
knew she was looking for a "particular building" and it
meant taking initiative and asking directions. She was the
one who went ahead to ask questions while her friends
waited in the car. She reflected that all significant moves
in her life had involved her separating herself from a
group and taking some initiative on her own. She also
knew from past experience that she could be looking for
something (i.e., a change in her life), and not notice that
it was "right there." When she found what she was looking for she knew for certain, "This is it!" There was no
doubt in her mind that she had found the building (i.e.,
project) she was looking for. What had surprised her in
the dream was that she had to leave the city to find it, and
the road to it was rough and bumpy. She remarked that
the thick carpet on the floor of the new building which
was ready for occupancy made it O.K. to fall down in
there.

Anyone listening to this dream can probably discover
some meaning in it. Not everyone would get a clear sense
of what the "new building" was for, or how they might go
about finding it, but each person can use it as a kind of
projective screen. The thing to remember when sharing reactions to dreams in a group is to take responsibility for

whatever you say. Prefacing your comments with the phrase, "If that were my dream, I would feel . . . ," or, "For me the image of the country road evokes . . ." helps remind the dreamer and yourself that you are offering personal responses rather than trying to tell him or her what something means. Everything in a dream takes its meaning from the context of one's life, and it is always the dreamer who is the best intuitive interpreter of his or her dream, regardless of how much anybody else knows about symbols and their interpretations.

The elusive nature of dreams, like intuition, requires that in order to learn from them we must be willing to take time to give them attention. Dreams often contain the seeds of future possibilities, and reflect what is unfolding from within us in our lives. If you take your dreams seriously and begin to record them regularly, you may find an increasing incidence of precognitive dreams and psychic dreams. Did you ever have a *déjà vu* experience in which you suddenly had a flash of having already experienced what is happening in the moment at some other time? Or have you ever come to a place for the first time, knowing rationally that you have never seen it before, and found it familiar? Some of these experiences can be explained by precognition in dreams, which gives one a glimpse of future events.

I have personally had a number of precognitive dreams, none of them very spectacular, but some quite detailed and clear. The most recent one was a few weeks ago when I dreamed of being in a large dining hall which had an unusual angular shape, windows with small panes of glass, and wooden tables. I wrote it down and remembered it clearly. About ten days later, I went to a woodland camp which I had never seen before, to a meditation retreat. The dining room there was identical to the one in my dream.

Arthur Hastings, a researcher in parapsychology who has been keeping detailed records of his dreams for several years, recently published an article entitled "Dreams of future events: precognitions and perspectives," in which he relates his own experience:

> As I observed my dreams and attempted to work with them and incorporate their perspectives into my waking life, I realized that for certain kinds of events, they were presenting what was going to happen and also what I needed to do about it. These were especially events in which I was to play some professional role—a lecture I was to give, organizing and conducting a seminar, a business enterprise for which I was a consultant.
>
> On one occasion I was to introduce a speaker at a lecture series in San Francisco. Four nights before I had dreamed that at the lecture the microphones did not work, requiring me to get the custodian. At the lecture itself, the microphones did present problems, and the amplifier picked up a speaker elsewhere in the building, requiring the services of the custodian to readjust them. The dream suggested what was to happen and indicated that my role was to find the custodian. The identity of the dream event—a lecture—and the waking event were the same in that case.
>
> Usually my dreams give a useful metaphorical view of a coming event, such as when I was planning a seminar for a group of presidents of business companies. A dream a few days before the meeting had me visiting with Arab sheiks in a desert tent. That dream suggested to me my feelings, and allowed me to consider how I would relate to persons who were like sheiks.
>
> On another occasion, I was director of a month-long seminar on consciousness research. Three nights before the program opened I dreamed I was about to go on stage to do a magic show, but I did not have my tricks arranged. I easily understood that dream to be a reflection that I did not have my act together. So I set about organizing my thoughts and plans for the program. I use dreams as a way of expanding my awareness of the possibilities of a situation and of responding to that potential.[23]

Many instances of precognitive and telepathic dreams have been reported elsewhere.[24,25,26] The elusive quality of the phenomena make it extraordinarily difficult to appraise scientifically. These difficulties, however, need not deter individuals from careful observation of personal experience. Dr. Hastings' self-observation is a good example of learning to make good use of an awareness of precognitive elements in dreams. Occasionally, a striking precognitive or telepathic dream may startle one into greater awareness, even when no deliberate effort has been made to remember or record such dreams. About a year ago, a friend recounted having such a dream. He dreamed that he was sitting in his study when Anthony Sutich, a mutual friend, and founder of the *Journal of Transpersonal Psychology*, walked in, looking radiant. This was rather surprising, since Tony had been paralyzed for many years. When he commented on being surprised and glad to see him, Tony replied, "Well, I'm dead, you know." The next day he received a telephone call informing him that Tony had indeed died just after midnight the previous night.

Such experiences do not need an explanation in terms of a belief system. It is enough to know that they occur, and that they sometimes happen unexpectedly. You do not have to be afraid of them, but you may find it useful to expand your awareness of them. Here again, intuition operates to let you know something even if you cannot figure out how you know. By accepting it, you can probably expand it. Maintaining an attitude of alert, nonjudgmental observation can help you increase the availability of such experience without giving it undue significance or attempting to explain it away. If you have precognitive dreams which you find disturbing, you may want to find someone to talk them over with. Beware of interpretations or beliefs which add to their mystification, or which dismiss them altogether as unreal. In working with any type of dream, remember that you are the best interpreter of your own dream, and learn to trust your intuition.

If you are aware of your capacity for dreaming precognitively, you may wonder whether you can do anything to change something you are afraid of or do not like. One woman, who had many psychic dreams and found them rather disturbing, was particularly concerned after she had dreamed that her son, who was in another part of the country, was in an automobile accident. Three days later he telephoned from the hospital. The accident had occurred just as she had dreamed it, two days later. This woman felt frustrated because her son did not believe that her dreams were precognitive, and said she was overprotective and unnecessarily worried. Whenever she warned him of something from her dreams, he suggested that it was wishful thinking or that she was trying to "make it happen." Under such circumstances, the ego tries very hard to take control and either deny the reality that presents itself in a dream, or design some more desirable turn of events. Usually, neither one works. The problem is more complex in that unconscious as well as conscious personality factors are involved. The unconscious and the dream world do not respond well to authoritarian demands. Dreams tell what one needs to know, not necessarily what one would like to know. Dreams can also help one confront the reality of a situation that may sometimes be frightening or distasteful. The expansion of intuitive knowledge depends on the willingness to know and understand more, even when it means being afraid or uncomfortable.

Although it may be possible to change conditions in order to avoid occurrences that dreams have warned of, the most effective work is on oneself. Changing yourself is the most direct route to changing your life. However, here again we are confronted with the paradox that wanting and trying to change can be an obstacle to change itself. Bear in mind that some of the most profound transformations begin with self-acceptance and awareness, which includes acceptance of dreams *as they are*. If they are frightening, then it is fear that needs to be confronted. Dreaming about a disaster that subsequently happens does not mean that you created the disaster; it means that you had an intuitive awareness of events which had not yet occurred in time. In working with inner reality, it is enough to take responsibility for your own life. Beware of feelings of power that lead you to believe that you can manipulate another person's life. The best rule of thumb is to let it be. Most of us have enough trouble finding out what is good for ourselves, yet are still tempted to prescribe what is good for others.

The problem with determining whether a dream is precognitive or a reflection of intrapsychic events is that there may be no clear indication from the dream itself. For example, if you dream of a person dying, you may not be able to tell whether this means that the person will die, or no longer be a part of your life, or whether it represents a part of you that is dying or being transformed into something new. It is useful to remember that in dreams nothing ever really dies, and that you may at times dream of your own death. I have experienced dying in dreams in many ways. As an adolescent, I often used to dream of drowning. I have also dreamed of dying in a plane crash, being shot, and being run over by a train. Since one goes through many cycles of death and rebirth during one's lifetime, remaining conscious during a death dream rather than waking in panic can be a valuable learning experience. Some people who have consciously died in their dreams say that they subsequently feel less anxious about facing death *and* less anxious about living.

Often when one dreams of people who have died, their presence in the dream is just as vivid as when they were alive. Shortly after my mother died I dreamed that I had a conversation with her in which I knew she was dead and asked her to tell me about death. It was a meaningful dream for me because the interaction that I experienced in the dream with my mother was free of all the difficulties in communication that we had experienced during her lifetime. I felt completely reconciled with her. Some belief systems would suggest that in this dream I was actually communicating with my mother as a disembodied entity. I find such belief unnecessary from a psychological standpoint, since the effect of the dream was the same, regardless of whether or not it was a purely subjective experience. It could also be easily explained as a projection, having nothing to do with my mother as a separate being, but I did not feel the need to explain it. For me the dream was a completion of my relationship with my mother and an acceptance of her death. The emotional impact of such an experience is recorded regardless of cognitive explanations, and can thus be self-validating, as this one was for me.

Dreams are said to be *compensatory* in that they often present the opposite of what one consciously believes or experiences. When everything in life is well-ordered and seems to be satisfactory, dreams may be disturbing, and this is usually when one chooses to ignore them. On the other hand, in some cases of depression, dreams may offer a new vision of life which can turn the tide and open up new possibilities of response for the dreamer if he or she is willing to give dreams serious consideration.

The following dream marked a turning point in the life of a woman going through a painful divorce after sixteen years of marriage.

> I am walking alone along a mountain path, having escaped from a castle in which a threatening male figure lurked. Lions are fighting somewhere in the vicinity, and I feel apprehensive, but I must keep going. A shadow of a white lion crosses the path in front of me. I need every shred of will power to keep going. Perhaps if I keep going, I say to myself, I shall meet Aslan (a lion from a storybook who was a protective godlike figure). After walking for a long time I find myself in a meadow with lush green grass. Then I am in the woods, and coming toward me I see not Aslan, but myself. It is just an ordinary me, neither young nor old, neither pretty nor ugly. I embrace my double and feel a rush of positive feelings, but she does not want to be held too tightly. This was perfect. It marked the end of a difficult journey. I felt I was home.
>
> I knew when I awoke that this was an important dream. In the months that followed I realized more and more that I was getting to know myself for the first time.

The emotional impact of this dream was such that it needed no interpretation for the dreamer to recognize its value. The dream images seemed to speak for themselves.

Everyone dreams every night, and if one chooses to become aware of dreams one can tap a vast storehouse of unconscious wisdom even without interpretations. Dream consciousness is itself a form of intuitive, nonrational, experiential knowing, and thus increasing awareness of dreams is one of the most direct routes to increasing awareness of intuition. As a general rule, it is best to stay away from books which offer specific interpretations of symbols in dreams. Such interpretation interferes with the expansion of awareness by explaining away an image and thus diminishing its transformative power. By prematurely dismissing significant images you may lose the opportunity of treating the images *as if* they are real, thus giving them space in your conscious life. It does not matter what method you choose for working with dreams. Many books are available which offer information on dream work.[27] You can choose whatever method appeals to you. In fact, you already know everything you need to know to begin expanding your awareness of dreams. Dream work provides an excellent opportunity for trusting your intuition, and learning to understand the nonrational side of your nature.

If you choose to work with your dreams as a way of expanding consciousness, you may want to learn how other societies have used dreams. In American Indian cultures dreams are often part of the religious system. Shamans use their dreams in performing functions such as curing illness or divination.[28] Dreams and visions deliberately induced in puberty rituals are used to determine a person's life's calling. Various methods for dream induction, notably fasting and isolation, may be part of the ritual, but the different rituals lead to the same source of inner wisdom: the dream itself as the most reliable source of guidance in life.

The Senoi people of Malaya, noted for the peaceful and co-operative nature of their society, use dreams on a daily basis for guidance in personal and social affairs. Children are taught to share their dreams at breakfast, and to control their dreams by lucid dreaming. One of the basic rules is to always confront and conquer danger or threatening figures in dreams instead of running away from them. Dreams are an integral part of daily discussions in the village council, and the tribe's activities are largely determined by their dreams. Neighboring tribes attribute magic powers to the Senoi, who thus maintain their peacefulness despite the proximity of hostile neighbors.[29,30]

In many ancient cultures dreams were considered to be divine revelations. The Bible has many references to God speaking to man through dreams in both the Old and New Testament. The ancient Egyptians believed that divine powers were made known through dreams, and the art of procuring dreams and the skill of interpretation were greatly prized. The priests who possessed these gifts were held in high honor. The ancient Greeks likewise regarded dreams as instructive and inspirational. "In divination by dreams," wrote Synesius of Cyrene (circa A.D. 400), "each of us is in himself his proper instrument: whatever we may do, we cannot separate ourselves from our oracle: it dwells with us; it follows us everywhere.[31] Allusions to dreams are also abundant in the Koran, and the earliest announcement of Mohammed's mission came to him in a dream.[32] The Upanishads, part of the ancient Vedic literature of India, refer to dreams as an intermediate state between this world and another, in which death is transcended. In the dream state a person is said to be "self-illuminated."[33]

In contemporary Western society, dreams have been accorded importance primarily in psychoanalysis and depth psychology, which recognize their value for psychological health and well-being. In ancient Greece a person in search of a healing dream would go to the appropriate temple and wait for the god of healing to appear in a dream. Today the healing power of dreams has been largely relegated to the consulting room, but is now finding its way into the culture at large. Jung considered dreams to be an important bridge between conscious and unconscious processes. "The general function of dreams," writes Jung, "is to try to restore our psychological balance by producing dream material that re-establishes, in a subtle way, the total psychic equilibrium."[34]

Thus dreams also aid in establishing a balance between rational and intuitive functions. There is no need to participate in a formal ritualized vision quest in order to get guidance from your dreams, although you may choose to do so. Dreams are available to everyone every night, and can be a rich source of creativity and inspiration. The German chemist Kekule discovered the molecular structure of benzene in a dream; the French mathematician Poincaré solved mathematical problems in his dreams. The British author Robert Louis Stevenson made up stories in his dreams, at first for amusement, and later for use in his professional writing.[35] Musicians hear music, painters see paintings, and poets make poems in their dreams. Dreams bear the gifts one is prepared to receive. By making space in your life for expanded dream consciousness, you prepare the way for your own unique creative inspiration.

Attention to dreaming can also awaken levels of consciousness that give new meaning to life. Intuitively you may already be aware of the depth of meaning that lies hidden in your dreams. Learning to understand your dreams is learning one of the languages of intuition. When you bring the light of consciousness into the dream world, intuition is validated, affirmed, and expanded.

6

Practical Problem Solving

To the rationally minded the mental processes of the intuitive appear to work backward. His conclusions are reached before his premises.

—FRANCES WICKES: *The Inner World of Childhood*

Intuition in problem solving applies to many fields of human endeavor, and can be classified as intuition operating at the mental level. As noted in Chapter 2, some studies of intuition in problem solving assume that intuition is a form of inference, closely related to subliminal perception. Others assume that intuition operates as extrasensory perception and does not depend on sensory input. In one study where creativity and task complexity were related to intuitive vs. analytical problem solving, the investigators concluded that the relative effectiveness of each mode depends on both the nature of the problem and the cognitive style of the individual. One of their findings was that more creative subjects found intuition more effective for a complex task, and analysis more effective for a simple task.[1] Whatever the explanation or belief about it, intuition is widely acknowledged as being essential to problem solving and creativity in many different forms.

In science, where logic and reasoning are stressed as the essence of the scientific method, intuition also plays a crucial role. After an extensive study of the process of scientific discovery, Michael Polanyi, distinguished professor of physical chemistry and philosopher, observes:

> And we know that the scientist produces problems, has hunches, and, elated by these anticipations, pursues the quest that should fulfill these anticipations. This quest is guided throughout by feelings of a deepening coherence, and these feelings have a fair chance of proving right. We may recognize here the powers of a dynamic intuition. The mechanism of this power can be illuminated by an analogy. Physics speak of potential energy that is released when a weight slides down a slope. Our search for deeper coherence is guided by a potentiality. We feel the slope toward deeper insight as we feel the direction in which a heavy weight is pulled along a steep incline. It is this dynamic intuition which guides the pursuit of discovery.[2]

Intuition is not opposed to reason, but works with it in a complementary fashion. Typically, flashes of intuitive insight follow the exhaustive use of logic and reason. Physicist Fritjof Capra says:

> Rational knowledge and rational activities certainly constitute the major part of scientific research, but are not all there is to it. The rational part of research would, in fact, be useless if it were not complemented by the intuition that gives scientists new insights and makes them creative. These insights tend to come suddenly, and characteristically, not when sitting at a desk working out the equations, but when relaxing, in the bath, during a walk in the woods, on the beach, etc. During these periods of relaxation after concentrated intellectual activity, the intuitive mind seems to take over and can produce the sudden clarifying insights which give so much joy and delight to scientific research.[3]

Polanyi refers specifically to the function of intuition in mathematics:

> I have shown how all the proofs and theorems of mathematics have been originally discovered by relying on their in-

tuitive anticipation; how the established results of such discoveries are properly taught, understood, remembered in the form of their intuitively grasped outline; how these results are effectively reapplied and developed further by pondering their intuitive content; and that they can therefore gain our legitimate assent only in terms of our intuitive approval.[4]

Einstein also affirms the importance of intuition in his own work. Alexander Moszkowski quotes Einstein:

Invention occurs here as a constructive act. This does not, therefore, constitute what is essentially original in the matter, but the creation of a method of thought to arrive at a logically coherent system . . . the really valuable factor is *intuition!*[5]

Moszkowski expresses the view that in art, too, an intuitive act of discovery is involved. Beethoven is said to have "discovered" a fundamental theme and afterwards elaborated upon it. It is not uncommon for musicians and artists to report hearing or seeing their work as images, either auditory or visual, prior to expressing them or giving them the coherent forms which can be communicated to others.

Carson Jeffries, a physicist at the University of California, Berkeley, who is also a sculptor of some renown, remarked on his own intuitive process:

All of the good ideas (i.e., sudden insight into the understanding of a phenomenon I have experimentally discovered, or the mental invention of a new experimental method) I have had in physics came like this: I would be absorbed in the analysis of a problem and excited by a glimpse of a solution, but could not really see the solution, only the expectancy. At some other time, often while going to sleep or waking up, I would get a really good idea—so good that I would get up and jot down a few notes (sometimes symbols). Then I would write out the full idea the next day in my idea journal. Even while mostly asleep I was quite aware that it was a really good idea because it excited me and made me happy.

In the awake state, when I see something clearly (something I have been trying fruitlessly to understand), I sud-

denly feel really good—a warm, sensual body pleasure. I
think I also feel this while sleeping and this is what wakes
me up.

An identical process occurs when I am working on sculpture. A clear mental picture of a new sculpture or concept
comes in the same way as an idea about a physics problem,
and I also write it down. My idea journal contains notes on
physics and notes on art all mixed up in random order.[6]

Intuition in art is not limited to the creative vision or
images which are subsequently given form. The creative
process itself is guided by the artist's intuition that lets
him or her know when it is "right." A painter knows
when a color or shape in a painting is "right" by an intuitive sense of recognition. Artistically, one color "works"
and another doesn't. Unlike the mathematician, the artist
does not need to rationally justify his or her intuitive perceptions of what is "right." Yet the words which Polanyi
uses to describe the guiding role of intuition in science
can also be applied to art: "Our search for deeper coher-
ence is guided by a potentiality . . . It is this dynamic intuition which guides the pursuit of discovery."[7] And, one
might add, the creative effort in any field.

The lines between the creative inspiration of the scientist and the artist blur when we consider the role of intuition in the creative process. Here again, intuition seems to
work best when one is not trying too hard to make something happen. Hadamard tells us that most mathematicians who have made significant discoveries in their
field avoid the use of mental words, algebraic or other pre-
cise signs, and rely on the use of vague images in the process of invention, and that Einstein suggests a "combina-
tory play" of images as the essential feature in productive
thought in this field.[8] The theme of play emerges again
when Dr. Huston Smith, professor of philosophy and
religion at Syracuse University, writes of symbolic art:
"Between thought (which proceeds indirectly through
concepts) and intuition (which directly identifies) lies a

middle ground. We scarcely know what to call it. Symbolism? Art in its sacred sector? It uses the stones of earth to raise on its flatlands spires that point toward heaven. This middle mode of concourse plays while logic works."[9]

For Assagioli, one of the characteristics of wisdom is the ability to *play* with opposites.[10] Maintaining an attitude of playfulness may at first seem inappropriate for problem solving, but intuitive problem solving is basically a creative process, and is more easily activated when critical judgment is suspended. Expanding awareness to include a wider range of possibilities (i.e., awakening intuition to perceive those possibilities) can often be done playfully, as suggested in chapter 2. Imaginative play is a key that opens the door of intuition, and its practical value is readily visible.

This link between intuition and creativity is supported by Andrew Weil, who writes: "The history of science makes clear that the greatest advancements in man's understanding of the universe are made by intuitive leaps at the frontiers of knowledge, not by intellectual walks along well-traveled paths."[11] Time after time it appears that major human achievements involve intuitive leaps of imagination. It is the intuitive, holistic, pattern-perception faculties associated with the right hemisphere of the brain that break through existing formulations of truth and expand the body of knowledge. The stabilization of intuitive insights, and their usefulness to humanity, are subsequently determined by careful, logical examination and validation, but the original vision or insight is intuitive.

Another area where intuitive problem solving is valued is in business. Success for entrepreneurs and managers who are frequently called upon to make decisions on the basis of incomplete information depends to a large extent on their capacity for intuitive decision making. It is their ability to arrive at *correct* decisions combined with a willingness to take risks that determines the success of their enterprises.

In the business world the use of intuition is usually called "playing your hunches" or "following a gut feeling." Decision making necessarily goes beyond factual data, as does economic forecasting. Arthur Hastings, parapsychologist and management consultant, maintains that psychic abilities can be put to work, and that executives make better decisions when they learn to relax more. In his management training seminars he trains highly motivated, energetic executives in techniques of relaxation, teaching them to sit quietly for ten minutes, with eyes closed, breathing deeply, relaxing muscles. Creative ideas can then start bubbling up and solutions to problems which have been elusive can come into focus.

Everyone is involved in intuitive problem solving in some way. You don't have to be a high-powered business executive to have to make decisions on the basis of limited information. Whenever you make choices which affect the course of your life (and all choices do this to some extent), you are calling upon your intuitive faculties. When you take responsibility for designing your own life, you are continually called upon to make choices without knowing precisely what the outcome will be. Major decisions in life are seldom rational, and decisions based solely on reason may not even be desirable. An intuitive choice of a marriage partner, for example, may develop into a more successful marriage than a rational choice which ignores unconscious factors. One woman in an intuition workshop who felt comfortably at ease with her intuition in this respect, recounted the following experience:

> The most important intuitive experience I've had in my life was the day I heard a voice in myself proclaim that the man I was sitting across from would become my husband. At that time I did not know Ralph well, though we were acquainted. I had no plans for marriage, let alone marriage to Ralph. Yet the day we shared lunch after a two-year lapse of contact was a fateful one for me. As he sat across from me recounting his experiences with a person on a plane, I heard a voice behind and to my left that said, "That man is

to be your husband." I responded by almost laughing. Ralph interrupted his story and questioned my mirth. I informed him I was reluctant to propose at that moment. We left the restaurant at some level already committed to a marriage now six years old.

Not everyone can point to such a clear sense of intuitive awareness in making this kind of decision. But many people, when asked to reflect on the turning points and important decisions in their lives, will recognize the intuitive factors that played a part in choices that changed the course of their lives. Another woman who had left a teaching job in Wisconsin to move to California with her husband was very discouraged when she found no jobs available in the town where they had settled. As they drove around looking for a place to live she was feeling disappointed and depressed.

I had strong feelings of unhappiness and disappointment, which I decided to keep to myself. Finally when we checked into a motel I jokingly suggested that I should have at least inquired about a job while we were in Riverside, where we had visited a friend the day before. I then went to a phone booth and decided to call out of curiosity. I think I was so down that I felt anything was worth a try. Riverside did have a few openings. They wanted a personal interview the next morning. My body was revitalized. I just knew that if I went for the interview I would have the job. My husband was skeptical, but I assured him of my positive feelings. I knew I could fill the job. We packed up and left within an hour. I had my interview and one week later I was teaching in Riverside. I did act differently because of my intuition. Ordinarily, I probably would have stayed where we were and found some sort of job rather than suggest a move. But I just knew there would be a job in Riverside for me. From that experience I learned it is better to follow intuition than ignore it.

A man who also moved with his family to California without knowing where he would find a job realized that intuition had played an important part in his decision to settle in Santa Rosa. Reflecting on his experience he writes:

> Upon arrival in California, we began to look around, not only at schools (my wife and I are both teachers), but also at communities, for our two daughters were still in school. I was offered two different positions, but we were not satisfied with the community in which they were located. One day, as we approached the city of Santa Rosa, a good feeling came upon both of us. At the time I would have called it a hunch, but somehow, this looked like a good place to call home. We stopped in at the school district office. They were interviewing that afternoon, so I went in and was later offered a position. Since that time, things in our family have worked out well. The thing that I can remember in regard to this experience was that I acted on my intuition.

Sometimes intuition can be very specific in providing solutions to problems, yet retain the quality of knowing without knowing *how* one knows. When asked to write about an intuitive experience in one of my classes, a student reported her experience in a high school algebra class:

> I was a low B student. I was confused and ill at ease in the class. I didn't understand what was going on, and each day when I walked into the room I felt painfully embarrassed. Then one day we were given an objective, citywide test, and I scored highest in our school, and third highest in the city. When taking the test I was aware that I couldn't figure out the problems and I felt defeated before it began. I resigned myself to failure and decided to go ahead and guess at the answers. As I was guessing I realized that I could just tell which one was the right answer out of three or four possibilities. I felt good and relaxed after I got into the test and decided to give up trying to figure out the answers. I had been extremely tense, and sweating profusely. I relaxed, felt my stomach muscles unknot, and felt almost giddy with laughter. When the test results were announced I was shocked, embarrassed, and pleased. I felt confused and scared at the results. How could I have guessed that well? What was I going to do now when the teacher expected me

to do better? What had I done to make myself so visible and to put myself in such an impossible situation? I felt the whole thing was a big joke, and I did not believe the experience. However, I did learn that when I didn't know answers on tests I could just let go, relax, and guess or write down whatever came into my head, and I often was right. I began to realize almost unconsciously that the answers are all there already if I can just tap into them somehow. I have never counted on being able to get practical answers of facts, but I do sometimes try to just let go and let the right answer for what I ought to do or decide come to me. If I don't listen to the answer that comes to me and make a different decision, however reasonably, I often get into trouble.

In contrast to the form of intuition that provides this type of specific information, there is another less well-defined form that intuition takes in shaping one's life. The less specific intuitive awareness expressed by Natalie Rogers in the following paragraph, can have profound and far-reaching effects on one's growth and development. Writing about her own experience entitled "Opening," she says:

To some people it may seem strange that I talk about the polarities within me, or the right/left sides of me. To others it will connect with their own experience. It is the continuous dialogue between these two aspects of myself that is much of my source for creativity. If one side of me totally dominated the other aspects of me—that is when I would begin to worry about myself. If I should become all logical, linear in thinking, pragmatic, moralistic, and stern, I would find myself single-minded and dull. If I were predominantly intuitive, receptive, sensual, and spiritual I would feel ungrounded, spacey, and strange. It is the occasional face-to-face confrontation of both parts of myself that stir deep excitement within. Instead of asking myself, "Which shall I be?" I am learning to ask myself, "What will I be if I push my boundaries in both directions?"

Becoming aware of the importance of intuition as a way of knowing is one of the most important elements I am learning in this opening process. The fantasy journeys and dreams are becoming important in my life as a valid way of understanding and learning. When I made the decision to move from the East Coast to the West, intuition and dream life played some part in the process. More and more I trust this intuition and pay heed to that part of me.[12]

Before reading further, take some time to reflect on your own process of creative inspiration and problem solving. Do you worry endlessly about apparently insoluble problems? Do you make a space in your life for jotting down creative ideas? Or do you discount your own flashes of insight as too insignificant or uninspired to be worth noting? You do not have to be a creative genius to unlock your own creative potential. Learning to tune in to your intuitive flashes is an integral part of getting in touch with more of the possibilities that exist for you, regardless of what your occupation or your interests may be. If you are not satisfied with your own intuitive problem-solving ability, the first step in changing or improving it is to be conscious of what you are doing. How do you close off possibilities? How do you shut down and turn off your intuition? Are you a wild guesser who acts impulsively without stopping to use your sense of discrimination? Are you continually distracted by following unrealistic possibilities? Or are you afraid to take risks and try new solutions? Do you always think of the reasons why your ideas won't work? Each person has his or her own way of closing down creative possibilities that are potentially available. In order to make the best use of the exercises in this chapter and get the most out of your attempts at intuitive problem solving, first take some time to become more aware of your own internal process. You know better than anyone else how you stop yourself from expanding the use of your intuition. Begin to notice what you do when you are confronted with a problem to be solved or a decision to be made. Becoming conscious of your own behavior patterns gives you the freedom to change them. Likewise, awareness of inner processes also facilitates change.

Take a few minutes now to think about your life and

remember the last time you felt truly inspired. Try to remember as clearly as you can what the circumstances were that led up to that moment when you felt you *knew* exactly what you wanted to do. Did the inspiration come to you in the form of a vision? The inspiration might have been for a work of art or for preparing a meal, solving a problem, or designing a new project. Did you follow through on your inspiration? *How* something can be done is often unclear when the original inspiration comes through. Did the *how* turn out to be so difficult that you abandoned the original inspiration? Or did you push through and surmount all obstacles to carry it through? Did you change your original idea in order to adapt to some external reality? These questions may be interesting for you to reflect on, and they are part of the secondary process, which is important in determining the actual effects of such inspirational experiences on your life. However, they are not directly relevant to the experience itself. In fact, being overly concerned with the practicalities of executing an idea can interfere with your receptivity to the flow of inspiration. People who feel their lives are uninspired do not necessarily lack the means of changing or implementing their intuitive inspirations. Often they are simply cut off from the creative source inside themselves that could give their lives a sense of intrinsic satisfaction.

Consider for a moment the turning points that have been decisive in determining the course of your life. You may begin by asking yourself this question: "Have I arrived at this point in my life as a result of my own efforts, or as a result of divine grace, karma, or circumstances beyond my control?" You will probably want to equivocate, but for the moment, if you were to take a stand on one side or the other, what seems true for you? What is the dominant mode in which you experience your life? From time to time your experience may change. There may be times when you feel you are at this point in your life because you have made specific choices and worked hard, and others when you feel that you are here simply as a result of circumstances, having had little or nothing to say about the way you have lived thus far. Either way, whatever beliefs you hold, intuition plays a part. As the function that takes you into the unknown, intuition always mediates your relationship to the future. Whether you consider your life's journey as one which is preordained and which you are simply discovering, or from the opposite standpoint, if you consider your life to be your own creation from moment to moment, intuition offers guidance and facilitates transitions from one stage of life to the next.

Imagining the Future

Given the awareness of intuitive choices discussed in Chapter 2, you can begin to visualize clearly whatever you want to create for yourself in the world. Of course, this does not mean you will get everything you want right away, but when you know what you want you are much more likely to get it than when you are unsure about it. Getting something you want often means giving up something you have. For example, if you want to feel good physically, you may have to give up certain habits of eating and drinking in order to make the change. However, if this is clearly your choice, and if it is truly what you want, it will not be as difficult as it would be if you were unclear about it.

A Zen story tells of a learned professor who went to a Zen Master wanting to learn about Zen. The Master invited the professor to have tea with him. Pouring the tea, the Master continued pouring into the professor's cup even after it was full, so the tea spilled out and ran all over the table and onto the floor. The Zen Master continued pouring. The professor said, "Stop. Can't you see what you're doing? The cup is already full." The Zen Master replied that the professor's mind was like the teacup. He could not hope to learn anything new when his mind was already full.[13]

When the mind is empty, free from preconceptions, intuition has the space to unfold. Intuitively one knows that change and growth mean letting go of the way things have been, yet it is difficult to let go of an attachment to the familiar, no matter how unsatisfying it is. This is part of a normal resistance to change. One can become attached to what feels safe and familiar and be reluctant and sometimes afraid to let go, not knowing what's next. Perhaps you have had the experience of holding on to an unsatisfactory personal relationship from fear of loneliness or simply not knowing what you would do without the other person in your life. One never knows for sure what will happen when a relationship changes. One may be happier or unhappier, or both. Yet intuitively you can be aware of what is best for your growth and development. Intuitively you may know what you need to do, yet be reluctant to act on it until you can rationalize it satisfactorily. Often the need for a rational justification takes the form of feeling that one has to explain it to someone else: "What will my parents, children, friends, colleagues say if I am unconventional?"

When you are considering possible courses of action, take time to relax and envision yourself as you would like to be five years from now. What are the qualities you would like to develop in yourself in the next five years? What would you like to be doing five years from now? Where would you like to be five years from now? Write down everything you can think of which would give you a detailed picture of yourself as you would like to be five years hence. Sometimes, when you think about the future you may not be sure about what you want for yourself. If this is the case, try the following symbolic fantasy:

> Take as long as you need to get completely relaxed and quiet your mind. Be aware of your breathing, and let go of any thoughts and feelings that come into your awareness. Get in touch with how it feels to be you at this moment. Imagine now that you are standing at a crossroads. Look around to see what sort of

landscape you are in, and back at the road you trav-
eled to get here. At this crossroads there is a sign in-
dicating where the different roads lead. Read the sign
and see what it says. Choose one of the roads and follow it wherever it goes. What is the surface of the
road like? What type of terrain do you cover? What
sort of vegetation do you see? As you travel down the
road you have chosen, do you meet anyone? What
sort of clothes are you wearing? Is there anything you
want to take with you? Give yourself plenty of time
to explore along the way, and to experience the place
this road leads you to.

This fantasy offers a good beginning for the use of fantasy in imagining the future. There is no need to interpret
in any literal way the imagery that emerges for you. The
meaning will emerge as you live with it, and your intuition
will give you some insight into your particular images.
Remember that images reveal rather than conceal psychological truth, and can show you what you need as well as
what you want. When I first tried this fantasy myself
about ten years ago, I had the following experience.

I was wearing comfortable shoes, jeans, a cotton shirt, and a
heavy, warm coat. I wanted to take some money along, but
realized that where I was going I would not need it, even
though I did not yet know where I was going. I took a
wineskin filled with water, and a cotton hat with a wide
brim for sun protection. When I read the sign at the crossroads I saw that one sign pointed to the city, the other to
the desert. I felt I must go to the desert, though it seemed
easier to go to the city. I felt that in the city I would continue to relate to people superficially, the way they apparently related to each other, and I had not found this satisfactory. It seemed safe and comfortable, but also hollow. I
knew the right path for me was the one leading to the desert. I took that road, and after walking for a while I felt
much too hot, so I took off my coat. I carried it for some
time, but I got tired of carrying it, so I decided to leave it.

I was reluctant to do so, thinking that I might need it later. I folded it carefully and laid it by a rock, telling myself I could come back for it, yet knowing I would not. Later I took off my shoes and my shirt, but kept them with me. By evening I had reached a rocky place and I slept under a ledge. I felt lonely and looked around hopefully for some sign of life, but none appeared. Next morning I set out on the road again, feeling tired and not knowing where I was going. The landscape changed and became increasingly brushy. After some time I came to a lake. The water was clear and refreshing. I swam and lay on the bank. It felt good to rest for a while. To my astonishment, on the other side of the lake I saw a unicorn.

As I reflected on my fantasy I remembered that visualization of a desert is sometimes interpreted as a symbol of alienation, and lack of feeling. Somehow this didn't fit for me. For me the desert seemed to be a place of inwardness and retreat. The choice I made at the crossroads was a deliberate withdrawal from social interaction. I remembered a description of the first step on the hero's journey as one of retreat from the external wasteland to the inner realm which contains the seeds of life's potentialities. This move toward introversion seemed to be a creative one for me. The desert promised solitude and retreat. The weariness and loneliness I felt during the first day of traveling down the road disappeared the next day. Leaving my coat seemed to be letting go of a symbol of security, and felt like a significant step along the way. Taking off my shirt and shoes seemed to be a willingness to strip down, though not completely. I still felt vulnerable and wanted to hold on to my protective coverings. The lake did not seem to be the end of my journey, but rather a resting place along the way, and swimming felt like a symbolic form of cleansing or purification. I felt a sense of renewal and refreshment, and very peaceful. My feelings about the unicorn were positive, as I knew it could be a symbol of Christ. It was clear to me that wherever my journey would lead, I had made the right choice at the crossroads.

It was not difficult for me to recognize the relevance of this fantasy to my immediate needs. I was at a turning point in my life, and after experiencing this fantasy it was easier for me to take time to get in touch with my inner life, and my own creative resources. It was not until several years later, however, that I actually faced a choice of going to a meditation retreat in the desert, or to a conference in a large city. I chose to go to the retreat, and it was indeed a valuable experience.

The outcome of this fantasy is not always as clear as it was for me in this case. The sign at the crossroads may itself appear incomprehensible, and be understood only after the road chosen has been explored. The fantasy also offers the opportunity to explore more than one alternative. If you accept the sign at the crossroads as relevant to your life at this particular time, you may want to explore more than one road leading away from it. However, making an intuitive choice in your fantasy and following it is good practice for learning to trust your intuitive capacity for making choices in your external life. Signs at the crossroads vary widely. Among those who have participated in this fantasy journey in my workshops, one person found himself choosing between love and productivity, another between spinach and ice cream, another between Austria and Hungary. One person took a basket of things along, but did not know what was in it. Another found himself carrying his piano on his back. All of these images clearly indicated to each of the persons involved what was happening for them, and what they needed to be aware of. Jung refers in his memoirs to the value of imagery in his life: "The years when I was pursuing my inner images were the most important in my life—in them everything essential was decided. It all began then; the later details are only supplements and clarifications of the material that burst forth from the unconscious, and at first swamped me. It was the *prima materia* for a lifetime's work."[14]

Given an awareness of intuition in problem solving, making choices, and shaping the future, one can begin to take responsibility for creating the context in which one lives. You may begin to see more clearly what you would like to create for yourself. However, being open to the possibilities that intuition can bring to awareness usually means letting go of specific ideas about the way life is supposed to be. In order to allow something new to emerge you may first have to let go of some preconceptions. You may be quite capable of making your dreams come true and getting what you want in the world by your own efforts, but once intuition is awakened you may find the nature of your desires changing. For example, specific material goals may become relatively less attractive, and the actual events in the melodrama of your life may be seen in a different perspective as you begin to recognize the patterns you have created for yourself, and see the possibility of breaking out of them. The future need not be a repetition of the past. Frequently one is caught by a paucity of imagination which conceives of the future only in terms of rearranging past events or experiences that are already known. Persistent attempts to explain the unknown in terms of what is already known, can lead to blind repetition of unsatisfactory patterns that limit growth and restrict possibilities. Imagining the future does not mean becoming attached to any particular object or circumstance that you want; it means creating a new context for your life. It is possible to create a context of trusting intuition, allowing all parts of you to respond as a whole to whatever problem or situation you need to confront. The context can be one of a balanced attitude that values both receptivity and activity. Remember that cultivating the receptive side of your nature allows your intuition to become more fully conscious.

Trusting the Process

When you work with imagery and apply it to specific problems in your life, remember that the imagery you consciously create reflects only part of what you want. Sometimes the imagery which emerges spontaneously, as in dreams, has messages that can tell you how to balance your perspective. If you are a person who is headstrong,

who knows how to go after what you want and how to get
it, you may need to cultivate more receptivity and acceptance. If, on the other hand, you have been a passive observer of life, having chosen not to exert your own will,
and you have allowed others to determine your actions,
the next step in your growth might be taking more responsibility for yourself, becoming more assertive and creating
the kind of life you really want.

Take some time now to think about a problem that you
are currently facing. It can be any situation, any unresolved question concerning relationships, work, growth, or
anything else that is important to you.

> The first step in this exercise is to formulate a ques-
> tion. Ask any question. In formulating the question,
> make it as clear as possible. What is the question you
> want to resolve? When you have a question clearly in
> your mind, write it down, or make a note of it so that
> it is clearly stated in your mind. The next step in this
> exercise is to begin your relaxation practice. Focus
> your awareness on your body. Take your awareness up
> to the top of your head and move it slowly down over
> your whole body, penetrating deeply inside your body,
> as well as moving it over the surface of your skin.
> Take as long as you want. When you have focused
> your awareness, and your mind is quiet, remember the
> question that you posed earlier. There is nothing you
> have to do about the question; just hold it in your
> awareness.
>
> Imagine now that you are at the shore of a large
> body of water. You get into a small boat and settle
> comfortably down with a blanket. The boat begins to
> drift away from shore and is carried gently by the cur-
> rent in the water further and further from the shore.
> Listen to the sound of the water lapping against the
> sides of the boat and imagine the rocking motion of
> the gentle current as you drift slowly further and fur-
> ther away. There is no cause for worry or anxiety be-

cause the current will carry you where you need to go. After a time you notice that the light is fading and you see that you have drifted into an underground passage. It gets darker and darker but the movement of the water continues and you drift along feeling quiet and peaceful. After some time you see a light in the distance and you realize that your boat is being carried toward the light. The light becomes brighter and brighter as you get closer to it. The intensity is almost unbearable. Finally your boat emerges into brilliant sunshine and you find yourself on a gently moving stream in a beautiful quiet meadow. The boat comes to a stop and you get out on the bank of the stream. In this place someone or something will bring you a message. The message may not seem to answer the question you asked, but don't worry about that. Trust that it will tell you something you need to know for the solution to your problem. Allow yourself to be quiet and still and wait for whatever image or message comes to you. When you have heard or seen whatever it is that is there for you, get back in the boat and turn on the motor. Very quickly you will find yourself back at the shore where you started. You can leave the boat now and bring your awareness back to the present time and place, to your physical body, feeling comfortable and relaxed. Take a few minutes now to write down what happened in the meadow. If there was anything you heard, anything you saw, write it down. It may not make sense at the moment, but something of value to you can emerge from it.

One woman who tried this exercise was wrestling with the question of whether or not she should get pregnant and have a baby. She experienced herself in the meadow in the role of mother, with a small infant. The image was so clear, and she experienced such overwhelming feelings of love, that the question was no longer a problem for her. She knew for certain, at that moment, that the right decision for her was to have a child. Subsequently she did get pregnant and have a baby, and was truly satisfied with her choice. The imagistic experience allowed her to let go of doubts and resistances that she had been feeling in making the choice.

Frequently when one is faced with a problem or a decision to be made, one is afraid of making the wrong choice. It is sometimes useful to realize that there is usually no right or wrong choice, it is simply a matter of preferring the results of one choice over another. Rarely is the outcome measurable in terms of right or wrong, good or bad. There is a well-known Zen story that illustrates this point:

> A farmer who had just acquired a stallion came to the Zen Master in distress, saying, "Master, the horse is gone, the horse is gone!" for the stallion had run away. The Zen Master replied, "Who knows if it's good or bad?" The farmer returned to his work feeling sad and miserable. Two days later the stallion returned and brought with him two mares. The farmer was overjoyed and he went to the Zen Master, saying, "The horse is back and has brought two others with him." The Master replied, "Who knows if it's good or bad?" Three days later the farmer was back again, crying because his only son, his only helper on the farm, had been thrown from one of the horses, and his back had been broken. He was now in a body cast and could do no work. The Zen Master again replied, "Who knows if it's good or bad?" A few days later a group of soldiers came to the farm as they were conscripting all the young men in the area to fight in a war. Since the farmer's son was in a body cast they did not take him.[15]

The story can go on indefinitely. One never really knows if circumstances or choices are good or bad, because one can never know all the ramifications. But one may certainly like the results of some choices and dislike the results of others. If one follows intuition in a conscious way, one frequently finds that one is guided to decisions which may not be rationally justifiable. For example, a person might turn down the offer of a job with excellent pay, because of an intuitive sense that he or she would not be happy in it. A person may choose to make a move, to go somewhere or not go somewhere, in accordance with a nonrational intuitive sense of what is best for him or her. In considering the choices you make for your own growth, be aware of your intuitive sense of what is right for you at a particular time. Your own inner imagery can give excellent guidance in making the choices which are best for you. The imagery of dreams, the imagery which emerges in states of deep relaxation, and the imagery which flashes through your mind's eye spontaneously at unexpected moments, all convey useful information. No one else can decide for you what you should or shouldn't do with your life. Your life is ultimately your responsibility. You can live it any way you like. When you acknowledge your intuition and realize how it operates for you, it becomes easier to trust it.

Many times one is faced with decisions where the reasons for or against doing something are equally balanced. Sometimes you may feel caught between two negatives, and forced to pick the lesser of two evils. At other times you may feel ambivalent when facing two equally attractive alternatives. The matter may be trivial, such as deciding where to go on a weekend, or serious, such as deciding which of two colleges to attend. You cannot possibly know all the ramifications of your choice. In the latter case there may be good reasons for going to each of them. Consciously or not, your intuition will play a part in the decision.

In wrestling with this kind of decision it is useful to get into a state of deep relaxation and visualize yourself two years hence, having chosen one of the alternatives. Notice whatever spontaneous images emerge if you imagine, for example, that you have chosen to go to College A. Then repeat the exercise and visualize yourself two years hence, having made the choice to go to College B. You may find that you have a different feeling about images that emerge. This may still not indicate a clear preference, since there may be positive and negative aspects to both images. However, in allowing your unconscious to participate in the process by means of imagery, you may be able to make a clear choice with confidence and certainty, with a sense of knowing what is the right choice, regardless of whether you can justify it or explain it in rational terms. You may not know until later why or how you were led to making a particular decision.

At other times, decisions may appear to make themselves. An intuitive sense of knowing what to do may be so strong that there is no question in your mind about it. This happened recently to Thomas Roberts, professor of education at Northern Illinois University, who came to California on sabbatical. He did not know where he would live for the year, but had often fantasized living on a houseboat in Sausalito, near San Francisco. While house-sitting for friends, by coincidence he heard about someone going away and wanting to rent a houseboat in Sausalito for eight months. He realized this his decision to take it was made instantaneously. Afterwards he found himself rationalizing the decision to himself, since it was relatively expensive. However, when he acknowledged that he had acted intuitively and accepted it, he experienced a release of physical tension that he had not been previously aware of. He attributed this to solving the problem of where he could live. No sooner had this happened than other things started falling into place. Ideas for the book he was planning to write suddenly jelled, and he could see clearly what he wanted to do and how to do it. He felt that his willingness to acknowledge and act on his intuition triggered a whole series of intuitive pattern perceptions that were of immediate practical value for his work. These events, in themselves, are not extraordinary, but subjectively they were all apparently linked to an increasing awareness of the role of intuition.

Sometimes this kind of clear intuitive sense of direction may be experienced as a powerful motivating force. In these situations reason must also be used as a mediator. A sense of mission or certainty does not guarantee infallibility or morality. Powerfully destructive personalities can be inspired by a sense of mission—a strong, intuitive sense of destiny. Much distrust of intuition is justified by historical examples of the negative potentials of following intuitive inclinations, without due consideration of possible consequences. Intuition does not evaluate. It indicates possibilities and provides insight into the nature of things. It is never a substitute for reasonable evaluation or moral consideration.

Various metaphysical systems that consider mind and matter intertransformable suggest that one can think of the universe as all spirit, with matter as its densest form, or as all substance, with spirit as its most rarefied form. In physical science this concept is represented in Einstein's equation, $E = mc^2$. Although all levels or planes of consciousness are actually said to be interpenetrating, visual representations usually portray the dense physical plane below, and the rarefied spiritual plane above. In this type of representation the continuum of consciousness is as follows: physical plane, emotional plane, mental plane, intuitional plane, and spiritual plane.[16] It is on the intuitional plane that one can tune in to the universal mind and thus gain access to any and all information available in the universe.

Itzhak Bentov, contemporary author, scientist, and inventor who describes the brain as a hologram,[17] asserts that it is on the intuitive level that all creative activity takes place. He points out that creative people rely more heavily on intuition than others, and says: "Intuition is a way of knowing without getting there in the linear, rational way we normally function. Basically, what we are doing is tapping into the reservoir of knowledge contained in the Universal Mind. It is already there in holographic form, so when a certain person needs a solution to a problem, the so-called intuitive flash may occur. This is a situation when people go into another state of consciousness for just a very short period of time—a second or two.

They go up into the intuitive level, where subjective time is greatly extended. So in a few seconds of objective time they can see the solutions to all their problems. They can understand them at their leisure and then come back—collapse back, so to speak—into objective reality."[18]

In the practical, ordinary, objective reality of everyday life, all faculties need to be brought to bear on decisions. One is ultimately responsible for what one chooses to do, regardless of how one arrives at the decision. However, since intuition, which is so often disregarded or mistrusted, is always involved in problem solving and decision making, it needs to be consciously acknowledged. Doing so increases the range of freedom in exploring alternatives, and can prevent one from getting locked into preconceptions. In learning to accept the wisdom and guidance of intuition in life, it must be continually evaluated in terms of the consequences of actions. As an integral part of the continuous change process of life, intuition is never static, and can never be completely dismissed. It can be repressed or ignored, but is always there to be reawakened.

7

The Wisdom of Intuition

> We are what we think.
> All that we are arises with our thoughts.
> With our thoughts we create the world.
>
> —THE BUDDHA: *The Dhammapada*

In both Eastern and Western spiritual traditions, intuitive knowledge is recognized as the highest form of truth. Western mystics and Eastern gurus agree that reason is limited, and only intuition can apprehend ultimate truth. The state which is called enlightenment or illumination is an intuitive experience wherein one penetrates behind appearances, to see things as they really are, to know them from within, through identification of the knower with the object known.

Sri Aurobindo has described this form of knowing: "One begins to know things by a different kind of experience, more direct, not depending on the external mind and the senses. It is not that the possibility of error disappears, for that cannot be so long as mind of any kind is one's instrument for transcribing knowledge, but there is a new, vast and deep way of experiencing, seeing, knowing, contacting things; and the confines of knowledge can be rolled back to an almost unmeasurable degree."[1]

Awakening intuition is inseparable from the development of self-awareness. Knowing oneself is essential to knowing anything about reality. Unconscious projections can distort reality to such an extent that when one sees one's reflection in the world, it is denied and disowned. In this way the individual separates him or herself from everything and everyone and becomes increasingly alienated in the world. As one begins to own projections, on the other hand, and sees things as they are, one begins to discover one's true identity. In this discovery one finds the guru (translated literally from Sanskrit as dispeller of darkness) within.

The willingness to follow the guidance of this inner teacher is trusting intuition. Behind fear, anger, depression, and anxiety is hidden the capacity for love, joy, serenity, and compassion. Behind all emotions is the wisdom of intuition that can lead one to the full experience of the central core of being. The more you are willing to open yourself to the full awareness that is potentially yours, the more authentically you can live your life.

A commitment to awakening intuition is a commitment to truth. It implies a willingness to listen to the still small voice which you can recognize as being true, even when you don't like what it says. It means a willingness to know yourself as you are, dropping pretenses and disguises no matter how successful your particular act may be in terms of getting approval from others. A significant shift from external to internal validation takes place as you open up more to an intuitive sense of what is meaningful for you.

If you are serious about wanting to fully experience the potential of both the right and left hemispheres of the brain and find a lifestyle that is truly satisfying to you, then you must give yourself the time and space necessary for allowing your intuition to come into conscious awareness. Remember, there is nothing you can do to make intuition happen, but there is much that you can do to allow it to happen. Be gentle. There is no need to force anything.

The regular practice of meditation is the single most powerful means of increasing intuition. Taking time to do the exercises in this book is a good first step, but once you have decided that clear intuition is a valuable asset in your life, you will want to continue to sharpen and expand your awareness of it. The silent mind, cultivated in many different forms of meditation, is the matrix of intuition. When you are in touch with the stillpoint at the center of your being, there is no need to use imagery or verbal exercises to activate intuition. It flows by itself, unimpeded by fears and preoccupations.

The wisdom of intuition does not follow the rules of logic. It will never make rational, discriminating choices for you. It is no substitute for careful research or data gathering. It is a purveyor of possibilities, not an evaluating faculty. Critical judgment may inhibit intuition, yet intuition never becomes a substitute for discrimination. Discriminating judgments are essential to making choices in the world, but let the mind be guided by reason, not bound by it. Your intuition can show you alternatives; it can give you a sense of what is possible for you. It does not tell you what is right or wrong, but it is a reliable indicator of what you need at a particular time. How you feel about trusting your intuition inevitably affects its functioning. If you value it and affirm it, it will flourish. How you think about intuition will determine how you use it, whether you bend it to egotistical purposes, or follow where it leads you. Pure intuition remains unaffected by thoughts and feelings, and will always take you beyond the boundaries of present conscious knowledge.

Intuition also takes you into those realms of experience that are ineffable (i.e., that cannot be expressed in words). Mystical experiences which validate the underlying oneness of life and transpersonal experiences which dissolve ego boundaries and expand consciousness beyond the usual confines of the ordinary waking state, are all essentially intuitive. Such intuitive experiences can give you a new appreciation of the spiritual nature of the deepest yearnings for love, peace, and wholeness. Through intuition the mind explores realms of experience beyond the reach of ordinary ways of knowing. According to Sri Aurobindo true knowledge is not attained by thinking. It is what you are; it is what you become.[2]

Writing on "Sufism and Psychiatry," Arthur Deikman tells us that in the Sufi tradition "The ordinary man is said to suffer from confusion or 'sleep' because of his tendency to use his *customary* thought patterns and perceptions to try to understand the meaning of his life and reach fulfillment. Consequently, his experience of reality is constricted, and dangerously so, because he tends to be unaware of it. Sufis assert that the awakening of man's latent perceptual capacity (intuition) is not only crucial for his happiness but is the principal goal of his current phase of existence—it is man's evolutionary task."[3] Dr. Deikman also points out that "Ordinary intuition, however, is considered by the Sufis to be a lower-level imitation of the superior form of intuition with which Sufism is concerned."[4]

In the Tibetan Buddhist tradition, Lama Govinda quotes from A Buddhist Bible: "The Buddhas and Bodhisattvas are not enlightened by fixed teachings but by an intuitive process that is spontaneous and natural."[5] "The Middle Way," writes Lama Govinda, "is neither a theoretical compromise nor an intellectual escape, but the recognition of both sides of our existence, of which one belongs to the past, the other to the present. With our intellect, our thought activities (and even our bodily functions), we live in the past; in our intuitive vision and spiritual awareness we live in the timeless present."[6] He goes on to say that in the realization of cosmic consciousness, "the problem of free will is dissolved in the rays of knowledge, because will is not a primary quality, which can be treated as an independent element, but it is the ever changing expression of our respective degree of insight."[7]

The more subtle the process, the more observation is likely to interfere or affect it in some way. In psychotherapy we find that becoming conscious of patterns of behavior results in change in a desired direction, without any attempt to *try* to change. In fact, *trying* is usually an indication of being stuck. Trying to make something happen is not making it happen. Trying to observe the mind is not the same as observing it. When you have learned to observe your own mind you will find that you can control it and predict what will happen. Just as one learns to predict behavior through controlled observation, one can learn to regulate and change internal states of consciousness through controlled self-observation.

Much energy is usually directed toward manipulation and control of the external environment and of other people. If you withdraw that energy from the external world and turn it inward to self-observation, you can discover how to transform your experience by changing not your external circumstances, but your state of consciousness. Recognizing the possibility of this type of control does not imply a value judgment. It does not imply that you *should* turn attention inward rather than outward or that you need to change your subjective state rather than attempt to change the world. Be aware, however, of the fact that one can do this, that internal and external control are equally possible. Just as one learns to control the environment through the application of knowledge, one can learn to control internal states by applying what is already known. Eastern spiritual traditions have, over thousands of years, developed remarkably effective methods for control of the mind. There is much to be learned from them, but this is not a substitute for what has been learned in the West. Intuitively we know that it is not a matter of either/or, but of both/and. It is always possible to think in terms of both/and, synthesizing and integrating all forms of knowledge to arrive at a deeper understanding of human destiny. It is possible for human beings to create the type of environment they would like to live in. It is possible to change attitudes and control physiological functions of the body that used to be considered involuntary. It is possible for you to design your life in such a way that stress is minimized and a sense of balance and harmony is maintained. Awakening intuition is only the first step on a long road of learning.

Self-awareness is the foundation of psychological health and well-being. To be sensitive to and conscious of how your body functions best, what keeps you healthy and makes you happy, is the beginning of taking responsibility for your life. You know better than anyone else in the world what you need. The problem in finding the answers you want is often not a lack of information but an unwillingness, or fear, of acknowledging what you already know.

Chogyam Trungpa writes: "No one can really change your personality absolutely. No one can turn you completely upside down and inside out. The existing material, that which is already there, must be used. You must accept yourself as you are, instead of as you would like to be, which means giving up self-deception and wishful thinking. Your whole make-up and personality characteristics must be recognized, accepted, and then you might find some inspiration."[8] As a teacher of meditation, Trungpa goes on to say: "Meditation is not merely awareness of practice alone, because if you only practice awareness, then you do not develop the intuitive insight necessary to expand your practice . . . we should allow the birth of an intuitive insight which really sees things as they are. The insight at the beginning might be rather vague, only a glimpse of what is, a very small glimmer compared with the darkness of the confusion. But as this kind of intelligence becomes more active and penetrating, the vagueness begins to be pushed aside and dissolves."[9]

Intuition can and does cut through confusion to show you what is true, but it requires willingness on your part to confront self-deception. How often do you pretend that everything is fine when in fact you feel awful? Or, conversely, how often do you habitually complain about things when in fact everything is O.K.? How often do you simply try to avoid the awareness of pain, be it physical or psychological, rather than do something about it? Intuition does not necessarily work in the service of the ego. Intuition may often indicate a direction that isn't what you think you want in the short run. For instance, someone who is feeling unhappy in a relationship may consciously want to change the relationship and keep it together, yet intuitively each of the partners may recognize that they need to go their separate ways.

Intuition does not always guide you to what you think is the best, or the socially acceptable way. "Ambition," says Ram Dass, "does to intuition what a weevil does to a granary."[10] With practice, however, it can lead through defenses and pretenses to the deepest sense of what is authentic for you. If you are willing to confront the fears that arise when you are faced with letting go of some cherished illusion, then intuition allows you to know things as they are. At this point, when you have made a commitment to your own inner truth, you may be increasingly willing to follow the guidance of intuition rather than try to use it to fulfill egotistical desires. The steady pursuit of self-knowledge leads eventually to a self-transcendence in which personal needs and desires are seen in a larger perspective. The intuitive realization that one is part of a larger whole, inseparable from the environment in which one lives, and that being is essentially the same in everyone, albeit in an infinite variety of patterns and forms, allows one to see oneself and the universe as an interdependent unit.

As you become increasingly aware of how you treat yourself, you will notice that you probably treat other people the same way. With this awareness you can become more conscious of how you create your own reality and how your attitudes and beliefs shape your experience. Belief systems, though chosen intuitively, invariably limit perception and experience. John Lilly, a pioneer among

Western investigators of consciousness, says: "Within the province of the mind what I believe to be true is true or becomes true within limits to be found experientially and experimentally. These limits are further beliefs to be transcended. In the province of the mind there are no limits."[11] To the degree that you are aware of this and take responsibility for the beliefs you have chosen, the possibility of transcending a particular belief system, or seeing your life from a different perspective, becomes a reality. Life itself can be a self-fulfilling prophecy. Your thoughts are continually creating the world of your experience. Only when you are willing to be wide-awake to the reality of who you are, to confront your fears and see the truth of yourself, can you be truly open to the many levels of intuitive experience.

Taking responsibility for choosing beliefs does not mean getting caught in a bind of choosing between opposites. The choices are not merely a matter of choosing whether to be more aware of inner experience or outer experience, or of choosing one possibility over another. Every experience offers the possibility of learning and expanding your intuitive capacity and inner wisdom. Intuition is not dualistic. The further you go in working with intuition, the more its wisdom will be evident in a balance and synthesis of opposites, in the harmonizing of inner and outer experience.

Inner and outer, the psyche and the universe, always reflect each other. If you change yourself, the world you live in will appear to be transformed. If you change the world around you, you will experience yourself in a new way. Both are true. Inner and outer are two sides of the same fabric. You can take responsibility for your own state of consciousness *and* for the way you choose to live your life. Developing intuition means staying wide-awake, being fully aware of your experience moment to moment, whether you are sitting still or actively engaged in work or play. Chogyam Trungpa says: "Meditation is not a matter of beginning to set foot on the path; it is realizing that you are already on the path—fully being in the nowness of this very moment—now, now, now. You do not actually begin because you have never really left the path."[12]

Learning to observe the flow of your thoughts and inner imagery, listening to your internal dialogues, and being aware of feelings and sensations are all part of the process whereby you can expand the awareness of being in this moment. By letting go of both external objects and internal fantasies you can also expand your awareness of the silent space in which all experience takes place. You can do this at any time, whenever you choose to focus on the context rather than the content of your experience.

Paradoxically, awareness of context can be enhanced by deliberate observation of content. Roger Walsh writes:

> As the internal stream of consciousness became more accessible it also became more available as a source of information to which I could turn at any time to find out what I was feeling, wanting, hoping for, valuing, fearing, etc. As my faith in this source of knowledge increased, I began to gain an appreciation of the saying "the answers are available inside," and also that the growth experience is one of recognizing what we already know. This sense of the presence of inner wisdom was very beautiful and resulted in a feeling of greater autonomy and field-independence.[13]

Finding your own answers through intuition may mean giving up old beliefs about the way things are and cherished notions about who you are.

The potentials of the mind are awesome. Sometimes one feels lazy, frightened, and uncertain in the quest for self-knowledge. Sometimes it seems easier to play old games, to maintain old images, unsatisfactory as these may be, than to risk stripping away the façade and seeing who one really is. Because of this, the commitment to awakening intuition requires relentless courage and a continuing willingness to face the unknown. It means accepting the possibility that the future may hold experiences that are totally new, experiences that go beyond the personal into transpersonal realms, extending to the infinite. The limits of inner experience are those one imposes upon oneself. Glimpses of infinite possibilities, however, may sometimes be so overwhelming that one prefers to shut them out of awareness. No matter. It is enough to attend to the experience of this moment, to be aware of your body, your feelings, your thoughts, and your essential nature.

Much work in psychotherapy is devoted to ego integration, to integration of the personality, to integration of the mind and the body, and to integration of inner and outer experience. This holistic perception of human life is first apprehended intuitively. One is whole, and one is a part of a larger whole. Yet in beginning the process of self-observation one often sees only bits and pieces, seemingly fragmented and scattered. Often the necessary task is to change perception and self-image rather than changing specific contents of consciousness or circumstances of life. When one shifts from the personal to the transpersonal level of integration, the self as context comes into focus. When one is no longer identified with the parts, one can see that expanding the context, changing the state of consciousness, does indeed transform experience. When the context is expanded, everything one does is affected.

Working on oneself and developing intuition are not alternatives to working in the world. Nor are they substitutes for rational faculties. On the contrary, they lead to a recognition that one is capable of both intuitive *and* rational ways of knowing. If one tries to change society without changing consciousness, one is simply rearranging the contents of experience. If one works exclusively on consciousness and abdicates social responsibility, one separates oneself from the world and again falls into the trap of identifying with a part instead of the whole. Like breathing in and breathing out, one needs both activity and receptivity. Exclusive emphasis on either mode becomes an imbalance. Awakening intuition depends on your willingness to see things as they really are, to know yourself as you really are, and to see the world as it really is, with all the beauty and all the suffering. Intuition deepens the experience of life in all its facets.

Intuitive awareness develops fully when one is able to experience who one is with a silent mind. The experience of enlightenment in Buddhism is said to come out of a silent mind, as an intuitive understanding of truth. The truth of this reality transcends anything one can say about it. Whatever is said may also be denied. Every realization contains the seeds of its opposite. To discover the reality of being is to discover that it is *no* thing. As *no* thing it is like a crystal mirror that reflects everything. The narrowness of perception hemmed in on every side by ideas, opinions, and bolstered by fear, rarely allows the experiential realization that out of this being that is *no* thing one creates the reality of experience.

Intuition provides the insight that sees through the filtering screen of thoughts, images, and feelings to the formless context of experience. Once you recognize the permeable, transitory nature of this screen, you can subjectively differentiate intuition from imagination. The distinction between intuition and imagination is precisely this: Pure intuition is knowledge that comes out of the experience of formlessness and silence, whereas imagination gives form to the formless and is conceptual in nature. When one imagines something, one is conceiving of it, no matter how abstractly. Thus, imagination is the vehicle whereby intuition finds expression in life. Many of the constraints and limitations in one's life can be attributed to lack of imagination. One seeks to attain only those things imagined to be good or desirable, and thus the failure to imagine alternatives may lead to depression and despair. Intuition makes use of imagination, dreams, fantasies, and other forms of imagery to enter conscious awareness, yet it remains distinctly independent of all these forms.

Pure intuition at the spiritual level is non-dualistic and non-symbolic. It is a state of imageless awareness, in which there is no duality between the knower and the known, between consciousness and its objects. This level of reality cannot be described in words, since words invariably posit duality, or separation from what is described. This intuitive experience of reality is not an argument that can be proved, it is simply a reality that can be experienced. It is the one reality which mystics of all ages and all traditions have pointed to, yet it remains unnamable. Anything one says about it, a Zen Buddhist would say, is like a finger pointing to the moon. The finger should not be confused with the moon. Ken Wilbur discusses three ways of pointing to this reality: The first is analogical, describing reality in terms of what it is like. The second is negative, describing reality in terms of what it is not. For example, it is non-dual, not time-bound, not limited, not describable. The third way, the way of the Buddha, is the injunctive way. The Buddha's teaching, according to Wilbur, was essentially a set of instructions for reaching this non-dual mode of knowing.[14] Tarthang Tulku, teacher of Tibetan Buddhist meditation in Berkeley, California, says it this way:

> We may have some idea that a place of ultimate understanding exists—but heaven is not necessarily somewhere else. It is within the nature of our minds, and this we reach through meditation. We just accept each situation as it comes, and follow our inner guidance—our intuition, our own hearts.[15]

Intuition is a powerful purifying awareness that sees into the nature of things, beyond duality, into the void, the matrix of all creation. With intuitive insight comes self-acceptance, compassion, and love. When there is no duality there is nothing to fear.

Who Are You?

Identity can be deeply affected by opening up to the level of consciousness characteristic of the intuitive mode of knowing. In this non-dual state the observer and the observed are no longer split. One identifies with what is ordinarily perceived as other. This inevitably alters the sense of oneself as a separate, independent entity. A shift in the mode of knowing, therefore, invariably results in a shift in one's sense of identity.

One way to get directly in touch with your own sense of identity in an intuitive mode is to clear your mind of all the preconceptions and ideas about who you are. You can do this by means of a very simple exercise.

> At the top of a blank page write the question, "Who are you?" and write down as many answers as you can think of. When you have exhausted the usual answers, keep asking the question repeatedly and continue to write down any free associations that come to you. You may also want to meditate on the question without trying to answer it directly, simply holding the question in your awareness, waiting for whatever emerges from the silence.
>
> If you prefer to work with a partner, sit opposite your partner and decide which of you will ask the question first. The person asking the question simply repeats the question, giving the other time to respond, preferably with a short, one- or two-word answer, rather than a descriptive paragraph. The question should be repeated continually for at least five minutes, preferably for ten or fifteen minutes. You may discover more about yourself if you continue for longer periods of time. When you have completed the time allotted, change roles and continue asking the question over and over again, giving the other person the opportunity to respond. If your partner draws a blank and says nothing in response to your question, wait a moment and then simply repeat the question. Stay with the question for at least five minutes, more if you want to, and then review the answers given by each of you.

How do you answer this question when you have

run out of roles and relationships such as student, teacher, mother, father, businessman, actress, etc? Who are you behind all the social roles you play? Intuitively you already know that *you* are not really the same as the things you do or the parts you play in life. The central core of you, the actor behind the mask, remains the same regardless of what you choose to do in life.

Another way of getting in touch with this central self, is to reflect on the totality of your life.

Take some time to relax your body and quiet your mind. When you are in a quiet, still, comfortable frame of mind, let yourself go back in your imagination to a time when you were a small infant. How did it feel to be you when you were a tiny baby, totally dependent on others to take care of your needs? What was that experience like for you? You may remember quite clearly. If you feel that you have forgotten, use your imagination to be there intuitively, truly identified with the feeling of being a small, helpless infant in the environment into which you were born. After a few moments, when you have truly absorbed the experience of being very, very young, go forward in your imagination to a time when you were five years old. How did it feel to be you when you were five years old? How did you experience the world when you were five? Take note of any pictures, images, or memories that come to mind as you remember being five years old. After a few minutes, go on in your imagination to a time when you were twelve years old. What was it like, being twelve years old? Do you remember what you worried about when you were twelve? What was important to you when you were twelve? What was your world like at twelve years old? What did you feel about yourself then? Go on now to imagine a time when you are twenty-five years old. What is it like to be you in the world when you are twenty-five? Going on now, imagine that you are forty years old. What is it like to be you at forty? How do you feel about yourself at forty? How do you feel about life at forty? What is most important at forty? Go on now to a time when you are sixty-five years old. What is it like to be sixty-five? Are you doing what you want to be doing at sixty-five? How do you feel about yourself at sixty-five? Go on now to imagine yourself being very, very old. Imagine that you are looking at yourself in the mirror. Take a good look at what you see and notice how you feel about yourself when you are very, very old. Who are you when you are very, very old? How do you feel about the life you have lived when you are very old? Imagine that you are looking back over your whole life, and think about what really mattered. Is there anything that you would have liked to do differently in your life? Are you ready to die? Allow yourself now to experience your own death in your imagination. Be aware of whatever comes into your mind as you try to imagine what dying is like. Allow yourself to rest now in the space beyond death, and in a little while imagine that you are ready to be reborn. You can be reborn anywhere, anytime, as anything you choose. What would you choose? Imagine now that you are going through the experience of birth, coming into the world for the first time. When you feel ready to open your eyes, take a few moments to look around and see everything as if for the first time.

This exercise allows you to experience both the continuity and the discontinuity of your sense of self. When you review the whole of your life and recognize that it is one consciousness, aware of all the different phases of life, both past and future, as well as the present, you can get in touch with the self which has no particular age and no particular physical characteristics, and nonetheless is you. The baby who is no more is just as much you as the old person who is not yet. Both of them are essentially identical with who you are at this moment. This awareness of who you are gives continuity to your life and can expand your sense of knowing intuitively who you really are behind all the roles, ages, and circumstances of your life. This exercise can also give you a renewed appreciation of the transiency of life. The young person you were and the old person you will be do not exist now. You are only who you are at this moment. All one ever has is the present moment. Yet you can project yourself into the past through memory and into the future through imagination, and when you wake up in the morning you remember who you are and think about yourself as the same person who went to sleep the night before and you make plans for what you want to do during the day. "The changing self," writes Douglas Wood, "*can* achieve unity in moments of intuition when time is perceived as an eternally developing present containing its own past or in moments of retrospection when a moment from the past lives again in the present."[16]

Another valuable thing about this exercise is that while it deals with both past and future, it actually enables you to let go of past attachments and future projections. This liberating experience can, at any given moment, counteract the tendency to divert too much attention to concern with the past and future. To the extent that one is filled with regrets, savoring past pleasures, or worrying anxiously about the future, one is distracted and not fully present. As one learns to live in the present, more and more energy becomes available for expanding awareness of what is happening right now. Only when the mind is clear is one truly capable of experiencing the fullness of reality at any time.

As you begin to know yourself and understand how your mind works, you may discover that you are not only your best friend but also your worst adversary. Frequently one blames others for the circumstances of life, refusing to take responsibility for oneself. But when you are willing to see more clearly how you contribute to everything that happens to you, you encounter another aspect of yourself. In most cases one is not an unwilling victim. Often one chooses to avoid confrontation, and consequently feels victimized by people or circumstances that one dislikes. When you recognize the adversary within you, the part of yourself that contributes to the situation, you can begin to take personal responsibility for change. Intuition allows you to see out of the inner prison you build for yourself, and only then can you make conscious choices about what you want to do. You may already know intuitively that you are your own enemy. Your resistance to change, your desire to hold on to what is familiar and already known, can cause you a lot of pain because change is inevitable, and by resisting change you create pain for yourself. Whenever you are moving into a new stage of growth, it is necessary to let go of where and what you were before. If you are forty, trying to hold on to being twenty-five, your experience is likely to be painful. *Letting go is essential to growth.* You may remember what it was like to be a sixth-grader, the top of the heap in elementary school. You were one of the big kids on the playground, and may have felt some sense of self-importance. Yet in making the transition to junior high school, you had to give up that position and go into the next phase of education, where you started again at the bottom of the heap, and all the big kids could pick on you. This familiar experience of growing up repeats itself in life in many different ways. Trying to hold on to achievements, attachments, or who you think you were gets in the way of further growth. Intuitively you know that your identity is not derived from any external possessions, roles, or relationships. Yet you may still cling to these things, these occupations, and persons that you think define you.

It is not only the inner adversary that you can become aware of through intuition. You can also become aware of the observer or inner witness, and of the higher self, the self that knows intuitively what is best for you, and that can be your best teacher, friend, and guide at any time. Very often, when you feel attracted to another person, you are attracted to certain qualities which that person has developed and you feel you lack. As this type of relationship develops, in time you yourself may develop some of those qualities. If, however, you let the other person carry those qualities indefinitely and neglect to develop them within yourself, you are likely to find yourself feeling dependent and continually threatened by fear of loss. Think about the different people who attracted you in your life. See if you can find within you the corresponding quality that may have unfolded. There is a common ground from which one creates reality, and as one learns more about that process, one finds that it is possible to evoke and develop desired qualities within oneself. Paying attention to those attributes in other people that you find attractive can be a useful indicator of what you would like to develop in yourself. Thus, by expanding your intuitive appreciation of others you can become more conscious of your own potential and allow it to unfold.

Looking at the various stages of growth in your own life, you may see how intuition has been operating, guiding you with that inner sense of knowing that has given continuity to the diversified activities in your life. Everyone has known pain and pleasure, joy and sadness. People often say that age twelve was a particularly painful time in life. The world seemed frightening, full of unknowns, and school was geared to teaching subject matter with little relevance to inner experience. The inner experience of intuition is usually not validated by society or peers or family in this culture, and as a result the transition from childhood to adulthood is often painful. Intuition is not encouraged, and anyone displaying unusual intuitive ability is likely to be labeled "weird." Many teen-agers who are troubled by frightening dreams or psychic experiences they do not understand have difficulty in finding a sympathetic listener. Parents who could be supportive may also be frightened by such experiences and offer little comfort or encouragement for further development.

By reflecting on your own life and the transitions you have experienced, you will begin to realize that inner experience is timeless. It makes no difference how old you are, when you venture into the inner world you are invariably confronted with the unknown, and learning to rely on your intuition is a valuable asset. It is not necessary to put off exploration of the inner world until the second half of life, although in our culture this is often the case. Learning to listen to the inner voice of awakened intuition is appropriate at every age. Everyone has a chronological age, and everyone is also timeless. The essential being who you were as a baby and who you are today remains always the same. You will inevitably go through many changes in your life. Your body is continually in transformation, replacing dead cells with new ones. Likewise you have the opportunity to experience the full range of human emotions as well as to exercise your mind in a myriad of intellectual pursuits. You will undoubtedly go through many transitions between birth and death, and feel differently about yourself at different times in your life. How do you feel about growing old? Growing old in a culture which does not value the wisdom and maturity of age can be frightening. Yet we know that aging is a natural and inevitable part of life, and letting go of the egotistical concerns of youth can be liberating. Letting go of the traumatic intensity of romantic teen-age love affairs, for example, gives one the opportunity to learn about deeply rewarding long-term love relationships. Letting go of trying to be what you thought you were supposed to be gives you the opportunity to be whomever you choose to be. Intuitively, you know who you are, behind the appearances you present to the world. The following exercise brings this awareness clearly into focus:

Take some time to write down nine words or phrases that define you. Put each one on a separate piece of

paper and arrange them in order of importance. Stack
the pieces of paper with what you consider the essential definition of who you are on the bottom, and the
one that seems least important on the top. Be prepared to take your time with this exercise. You can do
it alone, but it may be helpful to work with a partner
or a group with whom you can share your experience.

Take a few moments to relax your body and clear
your mind. You may wish to sit in meditation posture
with your spine straight to stay wide-awake and keep
your attention focused. Look at the words which
define you on the first piece of paper at the top of
your list. Allow yourself to experience fully what this
means to you and how it feels to be you, when
defined by this. Take it in, experience it, be it, for a
few minutes. Take enough time to acknowledge all
the ramifications of this particular self-identification.
Now turn that piece of paper over, and imagine how
it would feel to be you without that. Who are you
without that particular identification? How would it
feel to give that up? Allow yourself to experience letting it go as completely as possible. When you feel
you have let go, look at the next piece of paper and
think about the meaning which the second definition
has for you. Be aware of all the sensations, feelings,
and thoughts associated with this particular identification and experience it fully, as you did the first
one. When you are satisfied that you have experienced
it fully, turn this piece of paper over and let it go.
How would it feel to be you without that? Who are
you without that? Repeat this process with each of
the pieces of paper, giving each identification enough
time to be completely experienced and relinquished.
Notice how difficult it may be to give up something even in imagination. Don't be discouraged if
you find yourself resisting this process. Just be
aware of your resistance and let it be.

Do the exercise according to the directions with as

much depth of feeling as you can give it. No one will judge your performance. It is simply a way of learning something about yourself and who you are. When you have completed the process with each of the pieces of paper and you have turned over the last, most essential identification and let it go, take some time to experience how it feels to be you without any of the identifications you have given yourself. Who are you without those roles or attributes? Continue to meditate on the question "Who are you?" without attempting to find any answer. Let the experience be silent, nonverbal.

After a period of time that can be as long as you like, turn your attention back to the pieces of paper and turn over the last one you let go of and imagine that you are putting it back on. Take this definition of yourself back and be aware of your feelings as you do so. How do you feel about this particular identity? Very slowly, allowing plenty of time to experience each one, take back all of your identifications in reverse order. Notice how your feelings change as you take back each one. When you have put them all back on again, reflect on your experience of letting them go and taking them back. Who were you without them all? How were you different from who you are with them all? There is no right way to experience this exercise. It is simply an opportunity for you to discover who you are behind all the masks and definitions that you create for yourself in the world.

Among other things, this exercise is a way of beginning to confront your own death. Eventually everyone must give up all identities and self-concepts. It is frequently only when one is confronted with death, the realization of human mortality, that one can really begin to live life fully. Impulses toward spiritual growth frequently surface when the reality of death is acknowledged. The spiritual quest is for each person an individual journey guided by intuition. The road signs and teachings which serve to guide the seeker on the spiritual path are also relevant for the person wanting to expand intuitive awareness and self-knowledge.

The exercise described above may be experienced as liberating, or devastating, or both. Any transpersonal experience which involves the dissolution of ego boundaries and letting go of self-concepts is a kind of ego death that can be both ecstatic and terrifying. When you contemplate letting go of the usual models through which your reality is filtered and defined, and begin to experience the essential no-thing-ness of a transpersonal self, you are confronting the boundless depths of the psyche in which the totality of the universe is reflected. When you are no longer identified as *some*thing, becoming *no*thing, you simultaneously may become one with everything. The truth of this statement is apprehended intuitively, and it is intuition which carries us deeper and deeper into the mysteries of the transpersonal realms behind the masks of identity with which we shield ourselves from the overwhelming experience of the infinite.

Transpersonal experiences always involve an expansion of consciousness beyond the ordinary limitations of time and space and ego boundaries. The reality of these experiences is apprehended intuitively. One can try to describe them verbally or in writing, but the experience itself remains ineffable. There are no words which can fully describe this direct contact with reality, where the usual defenses are willingly surrendered.

In his research with LSD psychotherapy, Dr. Stanislav Grof found that all of his subjects transcended ego-centered psychodynamics and moved into transpersonal realms.[17] Jung foreshadowed current developments in transpersonal psychology when he wrote that the main thrust of his work was not the treatment of neuroses, but the approach to the numinous or transpersonal dimensions of experience. He wrote: ". . . the fact is that the approach to the numinous is the real therapy and inasmuch as you attain to the numinous experiences you are released from the curse of pathology."[18]

Today we know that many people have had transpersonal religious experiences which have transformed their lives. Many others have had transpersonal experiences outside of religious contexts, particularly since the popularization of psychedelics in the 1960s. Others have had spontaneous transpersonal experiences in the context of being alone in nature or as the result of a breakthrough in psychotherapy. Often, such experiences are not discussed openly, but are nevertheless a subjective transformation. At times a person may feel frightened or embarrassed by such an experience and try to deny it or discount it. Moreover, if the person is unprepared and lacks a context for integration of the experience, such experience may be disruptive rather than healing or liberating. When you have such an experience, you have a choice of whether to repress it or integrate it into your view of reality. If the experience is not integrated and validated, it does not necessarily support psychological stability. On the contrary, it may be unsettling and disturbing. On the other hand, when the experience *is* acknowledged and integrated into consciousness, it can have a transforming effect on your life.

Once you have become aware of the transpersonal dimensions of your own being, with the joy and certainty that intuitive knowledge affords, you can begin to experience yourself more consistently as the *context* of your life experience, instead of identifying with the *contents*. Thus you will no longer be totally identified with any one aspect of yourself. In psychotherapy, attention is often given to getting in touch with the body, with feelings and patterns of thinking. Owning and taking responsibility for yourself is a vital part of psychological health. Yet at the same time, as you learn to acknowledge and listen to your body, your feelings, your thoughts and images, you can also learn to disidentify from them. You have thoughts, but you are not your thoughts. You can, in fact, learn to control your thoughts, and you may even learn to quiet down to the point where they cease to interrupt the silence. You have feelings, but you are not your feelings. You need not be possessed or overwhelmed by your emotions. Feelings such as joy, love, peace, and serenity are potentially yours, just as much as feelings of anger, frustration, sadness, jealousy, and fear. Every conceivable emotion that is part of the human experience is potentially part of your own, if you are open to it. Often one limits experience, being afraid to experience negative emotions. One is afraid to trust intuition, because one would rather not know, imagining that remaining closed is being safe. Opening up to intuition implies opening up to the experience of life, whatever it may be. This willingness to experience whatever comes can be supported by the transpersonal awareness that everything is transient, impermanent, and changing. The stillpoint at the center of your being, the empty matrix of your intuitive experience remains clear and unmoved. It is in this core of your being that you can *know* what is true for you. From this perspective the intricate web of relationships in which we are all enmeshed may be perceived as pattern. In this pattern nothing is separate from anything else, and everything is interrelated. Thus, the non-dualistic nature of intuitive consciousness itself may be directly experienced.

It is actually impossible to talk about anything in a non-dualistic mode, since words themselves are distinctions which automatically exclude what they do not say. However, it is to this nonverbal, holistic, unitive consciousness that intuition leads. In Assagioli's words, it "apprehends a totality directly in its living existence."[19] It brings one into identification with the whole universe. Separations and distinctions, the contents of experience, and the formulation of ideas, take one back to the rational, linear modes of communication on which we rely whenever we use words to communicate. It is ironic that we should attempt to talk or write about intuition, yet it is in the translation from the intuitive to the rational modes of knowing that we may arrive at new syntheses which can further expand our conscious awareness of reality as it is. Life remains a mystery which continually draws us into itself. Intuition offers many new horizons in learning to solve problems, waking up to what we already know, and transcending boundaries of time and space as we ordinarily think of them. Finally, intuition leads always into the unknown, into the experience of reality beyond words, beyond seeing, and beyond knowing.

APPENDIX

Guidelines for Awakening Intuition

Many of these guidelines for awakening intuition have been discussed in the context of this book. Others are self-explanatory, and are simply summarized here as reminders of methods available.

INTENTION The first requirement for consciously awakening intuition is a clear intention to do so. Intuition is already within you, but to awaken it you have to value it and *intend* to develop it.

TIME Your willingness to devote time to tuning in to your intuition, making a space for its unfolding in your life, is part of valuing and developing it.

RELAXATION Letting go of physical and emotional tension gives intuition the space to enter your conscious awareness.

SILENCE Intuition flourishes in silence. Learning to quiet the mind is therefore part of the training for awakening intuition. Various meditative practices are useful in learning to maintain the necessary inner silence.

HONESTY Willingness to face self-deception and to be honest with yourself and others is essential. Creating any kind of smokescreen interferes with clear vision. Giving up pretenses is a big step in awakening intuition.

RECEPTIVITY Learning to be quiet and receptive allows intuition to unfold. Too much activity or conscious programing gets in the way of intuitive awareness that emerges when a receptive attitude is cultivated.

SENSITIVITY Finely tuned sensitivity to both inner and outer processes provides more information and expands intuitive knowing. Sensitivity to energy awareness and the quality of experience is particularly useful.

NONVERBAL PLAY Drawing, music, movement, clay, and other forms of nonverbal expression done in a spirit of play, rather than for the purpose of goal-oriented achievement, provide excellent channels for activating intuitive, right-hemisphere functions.

TRUST Trusting the process, trusting yourself, trusting your experience, are the keys to trusting and developing your intuition.

OPENNESS If you are afraid of being seen, you may close up and then be unable to see. Being open to all experiences, both inner and outer, gives intuition the space it needs to develop fully.

COURAGE Fear gets in the way of direct experience and often generates deception. Your willingness to experience and confront your fears will facilitate the expansion of intuition.

ACCEPTANCE A nonjudgmental attitude, an acceptance of things as they are, including self-acceptance, allows intuition to function freely.

LOVE Opening your heart to feelings of nonjudgmental love and compassion allows you to see into the nature of things. Emotional empathy and intuitive identification are facilitated by love and compassion.

NONATTACHMENT The willingness to let things be as they are, rather than trying to make them be the way you would like them to be, or the way you think they should be, allows intuition to emerge. You can see things as they are only when desires and fears are out of the way.

DAILY PRACTICE Intuitive awareness grows with daily attention. If you discount or neglect it most of the time and only want it to perform occasionally, it may not respond.

JOURNAL KEEPING Keeping a record of intuitive flashes, hunches, insights, and images that come to mind spontaneously at any time of the day or night, can help stabilize and validate them.

SUPPORT GROUP Finding one, two, or more friends with whom you can share your interest in the development of intuition, as well as your successes, failures, hopes, and fears, can facilitate and accelerate the process of development. Sharing experience with someone who is willing to listen without judging or interpreting, is very useful.

ENJOYMENT Following intuition does not always feel good. At times it may seem difficult and entail arduous work. At others times it may be effortless. Enjoying the creative resources of intuition is based on the intrinsic satisfaction of expanding consciousness, taking responsibility for your life, and surrendering to your own true nature.

REFERENCES

CHAPTER 1. TUNING IN TO INTUITION

1. *The Spectrum of Consciousness* (Wheaton, Ill.: Theosophical Publishing House, 1977), p. 69.

2. Sengstan, third Zen patriarch. *Hsin Hsin Ming: Verses on the Faith Mind*, tr. by R. Clarke (Virginia Beach: Alan Clements, 1976).

3. *The Varieties of the Meditative Experience* (New York: Dutton, 1977), p. 118.

4. Lester Fehmi, "Open Focus Training." Paper presented at the Council Grove Conference on Voluntary Control of Internal States (The Menninger Foundation, Council Grove, Kansas, April 3, 1975).

   This abridged version of the exercise is reprinted by permission of Dr. Lester Fehmi. For further information on open focus training write Dr. Lester Fehmi, The Medical Center, 905 Herrontown Road, Princeton, New Jersey 08540. A six-tape series, *Open Focus Training*, may be ordered from Biofeedback Computers Inc. of Indianapolis, 6218 Brookline Drive, Indianapolis, Ind. 46220.

5. R. Ornstein, *The Psychology of Consciousness* (New York: Viking, 1972), p. 163–64.

6. *Psychosynthesis* (New York: Hobbs Dohrman, 1965), p. 119.

7. Ibid., p. 22.

8. *Discourses I, II, III* (San Francisco: Sufism Reoriented, 1967), p. 191.

9. Wilbur, op. cit., p. 331.

10. *The Experience of Insight* (Santa Cruz, Ca.: Unity Press, 1976), p. 68.

CHAPTER 2. CHOOSING YOUR OWN WAY

1. Malcolm Westcott, *Toward a Contemporary Psychology of Intuition* (New York: Holt, Rinehart and Winston, 1968), p. 24.

2. "The Nature of Intuition," *Psychiatric Quarterly* 23 (1949): pp. 203–26.

3. Westcott, op. cit., pp. 119–48.

4. M. L. Von Franz and J. Hillman, *Jung's Typology* (New York: Spring Publications, 1971).

5. A Weil, *The Natural Mind* (Boston: Houghton Mifflin, 1972), p. 150.

6. Westcott, op. cit., p. 11.

7. Satprem, *Sri Aurobindo, or The Adventure of Consciousness* (Pondicherry, India: Sri Aurobindo Society, 1970), p. 191.

8. *Foundations of Tibetan Mysticism* (New York: Samuel Weiser, 1969), p. 74.

9. *Meditation in Action* (Berkeley, Ca.: Shambala, 1970), p. 29.

10. C. M. Owens, "Zen Buddhism," *Transpersonal Psychologies*, ed. C. Tart (New York: Harper and Row, 1975), p. 156.

11. *The Psychology of Consciousness* (New York: Viking, 1972), p. x, Preface.

12. *The Tao of Physics* (Berkeley, Ca.: Shambala, 1975), p. 131.

13. *The Medium, the Mystic and the Physicist* (New York: Viking, 1974), p. 100.

14. Ibid., p. 61.

15. "Bridging Science and Values: A Unifying View of Mind and Brain," *American Psychologist* 32 (April 1977): pp. 237–45.

CHAPTER 3. VARIETIES OF INTUITIVE
EXPERIENCE

1. M. Ullman and S. Krippner, *Dream Telepathy* (New York: Macmillan, 1973), pp. 13–14.

2. Ibid., p. 210.

3. "The Physical Universe, the Spiritual Universe, and the Paranormal," *Transpersonal Psychologies* (New York: Harper and Row, 1975), pp. 132–33.

4. *The Inner World of Childhood*, rev. ed. (New York: New American Library, 1966), p. 142.

5. R. Assagioli, *Psychosynthesis* (New York: Hobbs Dohrman, 1965), p. 221.

6. Tarthang Tulku, *Time, Space and Knowledge* (Emeryville, Ca.: Dharma Publishing, 1977), p. 66.

7. *Realms of the Human Unconscious* (New York: Viking, 1975), p. 155.

8. M. Bucke, *Cosmic Consciousness* (New York: Dutton, 1969), p. 10.

9. Swami Rama, R. Ballantine, and Swami Ajaya, *Yoga and Psychotherapy* (Glenview, Ill.: Himalayan Institute, 1976), p. 265.

10. R. Gerard, Workshop notes. Professional training in psychosynthesis: Intuitive awareness. Berkeley, October, 1972.

11. A. Dreyfuss and D. Feinstein, "My Body Is Me: Body-based Approaches to Personal Enrichment," *Humanistic Perspectives: Current Trends in Psychology*, ed. B. McWaters (Monterey, Ca.: Brooks Cole, 1977), p. 43.

12. Tart, op. cit., p. 134.

13. "Female Intuition Measured at Last?" *New Society* (London; 1977).

14. Elizabeth Herron, Unpublished paper (1976).

15. *Toward a Contemporary Psychology of Intuition* (New York: Holt, Rinehart and Winston, 1968), pp. 49–51.

16. *An Essay on the Psychology of Invention in the Mathematical Field* (Princeton, 1945), p. 142, Appendix.

17. G. Holton, "Where Is Reality? The Answers of Einstein" *Science and Synthesis* (New York, Heidelberg, Berlin: Springer-Verlag, 1971), p. 69.

18. P. Schilpp (ed.), *Albert Einstein: Philosopher-Scientist*. The Library of Living Philosophers, Inc. (Evanston, Ill., 1949), p. 131.

19. "The Structure of Creativity in Physics," *Vistas in Physical Reality*, eds. E. Laszlo and E. Sellon (New York: Sellon Press, 1976), p. 154.

20. J. Mihalasky, "Extrasensory Perception in Management," *Advanced Management Journal* (July 1976).

21. "Planning on the Left Side and Managing on the Right," *Harvard Business Review* (July–August 1976): pp. 49–58.

22. D. Goleman, "Split-brain Psychology: Fad of the Year," *Psychology Today* (October 1977): p. 89.

23. *Executive ESP* (Englewood Cliffs, N.J.: Prentice Hall, 1974).

24. "Dialogue: Your Most Exciting Moment in Research?" *LBL Newsmagazine* (Fall, 1976): p. 2.

25. E. Green and A. Green, *Beyond Biofeedback* (New York: Delacorte, 1977).

26. E. Green, A. Green, and D. Walters, "Voluntary Control of Internal States: Psychological and Physiological," *Journal of Transpersonal Psychology* (1970): pp. 1–27.

27. Assagioli, op. cit., p. 220.

28. *The Search for Existential Identity* (San Francisco: Josey Bass, 1976), p. 296.

29. *The Farther Reaches of Human Nature* (New York: Viking, 1971).

30. *The Spectrum of Consciousness* (Wheaton, Ill.: Theosophical Publishing House, 1977), p. 46.

31. P. Yogananda, *The Autobiography of a Yogi* (Los Angeles: Self-Realization Fellowship, 1969), p. 31.

32. *Sri Aurobindo, or The Adventure of Consciousness* (Pondicherry, India: Sri Aurobindo Society, 1970), p 192.

33. *The Medium, the Mystic and the Physicist* (New York: Viking, 1974), p. 154.

CHAPTER 4. IMAGERY AND INTUITION

1. E. Green and A. Green, *Beyond Biofeedback* (New York: Delacorte, 1977), pp. 33–41.

2. Ibid., pp. 33–34.

3. E. Green, A. Green, and D. Walters, "Voluntary Control of Internal States: Psychological and Physiological," *Journal of Transpersonal Psychology* (1970): p. 5.

4. Ibid., p. 14.

5. *The Natural Depth in Man* (New York: Harper and Row, 1972), p. 89.

6. "Bimodal Consciousness," *The Nature of Human Consciousness*, ed. R. Ornstein (San Francisco: Freeman, 1972), p. 68.

7. "Reflections on Psychotherapy," *Journal of Transpersonal Psychology* (1976): pp. 100–1.

8. H. E. Puthoff and R. Targ, "A Perceptual Channel for Information Transfer over Kilometer Distances: Historical Perspective and Recent Research," *Proceedings of the Institute of Electrical and Electronics Engineers, Inc.*, Vol. 64, No. 3 (March 1976).

9. *Man and His Symbols* (Garden City, N.Y.: Doubleday, 1964), p. 55.

10. *The Farther Reaches of Human Nature* (New York: Viking, 1971), p. 35.

CHAPTER 5. DREAMS AND INTUITION

1. *The Dream Game* (New York: Harper and Row, 1974), p. 27.

2. J. Jaynes, *The Origin of Consciousness in the Breakdown of the Bicameral Mind* (Boston: Houghton Mifflin, 1976).

3. D. Goleman, "Split-brain Psychology: Fad of the Year," *Psychology Today* (October 1977): p. 89.

4. *The Interpretation of Dreams*, 3rd ed., tr. by J. Strachey (New York: Avon Books, 1967), p. 37.

5. Ibid., p. 133.

6. Ibid., p. 137.

7. *Man and His Symbols* (Garden City, N.Y.: Doubleday, 1964), p. 53.

8. *The Dream—the Vision of the Night* (Los Angeles: The Analytical Psychology Club of Los Angeles and the C. G. Jung Institute of Los Angeles, 1975), p. 168.

9. Jung, op. cit., p. 50.

10. A. Hastings, "Dreams of Future Events: Precognitions and Perspectives," *Journal of the American Society of Psychosomatic Dentistry & Medicine* (1977): pp. 51–60.

11. M. Ullman, S. Krippner, and A. Vaughan, *Dream Telepathy* (New York: Macmillan, 1973).

12. Hastings, op. cit., p. 51.

13. Swami Rama, R. Ballentine, and Swami Ajaya, *Yoga and Psychotherapy: The Evolution of Consciousness* (Glenview, Ill.: Himalayan Institute, 1976), p. 135.

14. E. Green, et al., *Biofeedback for Mind-Body Self Regulation: Healing and Creativity* (Topeka, Ks.: The Menninger Foundation, 1971), p. 23.

15. *Creative Dreaming* (New York: Ballantine Books, 1976), pp. 118–150.

16. W. Y. Evans-Wentz, *The Tibetan Book of the Dead* (New York: Oxford University Press, 1960), p. 147.

17. *Dream Power* (New York: Coward, McCann & Geoghegan, 1972), p. 21.

18. E. Rossi, *Dreams and the Growth of Personality* (New York: Pergamon Press, 1972), p. 142.

19. *The Natural Depth in Man* (New York: Harper & Row, 1972), p. 110.

20. Ibid., p. 104.

21. Freud, op cit., p. 313.

22. J. Henderson, "Ancient Myths and Modern Man" in C. G. Jung, *Man and His Symbols* (Garden City, N.Y.: Doubleday, 1964), pp. 154–56.

23. Hastings, op. cit., pp. 55–56.

24. Ullman, Krippner and Vaughan, op. cit.

25. Jung, *Man and His Symbols*, op. cit.

26. R. Woods and H. Greenhouse (eds.), *The New World of Dreams* (New York: Macmillan, 1974).

27. Faraday, *The Dream Game* and *Dream Power*, op. cit.; Garfield, op. cit.

28. Garfield, op. cit., pp. 70–71.

29. Ibid., p. 83.

30. K. Stewart, "Dream Theory in Malaya," *Altered States of Consciousness*, ed. C. Tart (Garden City, N.Y.: Doubleday, 1972).

31. Woods and Greenhouse, op. cit., p. 160.

32. Ibid., p. 132.

33. Ibid., p. 126.

34. Jung, *Man and His Symbols*, p. 50.

35. Garfield, op. cit., pp. 37–58.

CHAPTER 6. PRACTICAL PROBLEM SOLVING

1. D. K. Simonton, "Creativity, Task Complexity, and Intuitive Versus Analytical Problem Solving," *Psychological Reports* (1975): pp. 351–54.

2. M. Polanyi, in M. Green (ed.), "Toward a Unity of Knowledge," *Psychological Issues* (International Universities Press, New York, 1969). Cited in A. Deikman, "Sufism and Psychiatry," *Journal of Nervous and Mental Diseases* (1977), p. 60.

3. *The Tao of Physics* (Berkeley: Shambala, 1975), p. 31.

4. *Personal Knowledge: Toward a Post-critical Philosophy* (Chicago: University of Chicago Press, 1958), p. 188.

5. A. Moszkowski, *Conversations with Einstein*, translated by Henry L. Brose (New York: Horizon Press, 1970), p. 96.

6. C. Jeffries, personal communication.

7. M. Polanyi in M. Green (ed.), op. cit., p. 60.

8. *An Essay on the Psychology of Invention in the Mathematical Field* (Princeton: Princeton University Press, 1945), p. 142.

9. *Forgotten Truth: The Primordial Tradition* (New York: Harper & Row, 1976), p. 89.

10. *The Act of Will* (New York: Viking, 1973), p. 104.

11. *The Natural Mind* (Boston: Houghton Mifflin, 1973), p. 150.

12. Unpublished manuscript.

13. Zen story recounted from memory.

14. *Memories, Dreams and Reflections* (New York: Vintage Books, 1961), p. 199.

15. Zen story recounted from memory.

16. E. Green and A. Green, "On the Meaning of Transpersonal: Some Metaphysical Perspectives," *Journal of Transpersonal Psychology* (1971): pp. 27–43.

17. *Stalking the Wild Pendulum: On the Mechanics of Consciousness* (New York: Dutton, 1977).

18. "Science Discovers Consciousness," *New Age Journal* (September 1977): p. 21.

CHAPTER 7. THE WISDOM OF INTUITION

1. Satprem, *Sri Aurobindo, or The Adventure of Consciousness* (Pondicherry, India: Sri Aurobindo Society, 1970), p. 158.

2. Ibid., p. 158.

3. "Sufism and Psychiatry," *Journal of Nervous and Mental Diseases* (1977): pp. 17–18.

4. Ibid., p. 12.

5. Govinda, *Foundations of Tibetan Mysticism* (New York: Samuel Weiser, 1969), p. 199.

6. Ibid., p. 271.

7. Ibid., p. 272.

8. C. Trungpa, *Cutting Through Spiritual Materialism* (Berkeley: Shambala, 1973), p. 64.

9. Ibid., pp. 179, 183.

10. Lecture at Naropa Institute, 1975.

11. *The Center of the Cyclone* (New York: Julian Press, 1972), p. 5.

12. Trungpa, op. cit., p. 203.

13. R. Walsh, "Reflections on Psychotherapy," *Journal of Transpersonal Psychology* (1976), pp. 107–8.

14. *The Spectrum of Consciousness* (Wheaton, Ill.: The Theosophical Publishing House, 1977), p. 58.

15. *Gesture of Balance* (Emeryville, Ca.: Dharma Publishing, 1977), p. 85.

16. D. Wood, "Even Such is Time," *Revision* (Winter 1978): p. 49.

17. *Realms of the Human Unconscious* (New York: Viking, 1975), p. 212.

18. *Letters*, ed. G. Adler (Princeton: Princeton University Press, 1973), p. 377.

19. *Psychosynthesis* (New York: Hobbs Dohrman, 1965), p. 217.

INDEX